IRISHPOLITICS
INPOSTCARDS

To Fidelma

from Declan

with best wishes

IRISHPOLITICS INPOSTCARDS

Declan Martin

ULSTER HISTORICAL FOUNDATION

First published 2016
by Ulster Historical Foundation,
First Floor, Corn Exchange,
31 Gordon Street, Belfast, BT1 2LG
Charity Ref. No. XN48460
www.ancestryireland.com
www.booksireland.org.uk

ISBN: 978-1-909556-44-7

COVER IMAGES:
Image 1: Londonderry under Home Rule; image 2: Home Rule 'Shipwreck'
Image 3: Dr Sinn Féin – Forcible Feeding.

Printed by GPS Colour Graphics Ltd.
Design by J. P. Morrison

CONTENTS

LIST OF ILLUSTRATIONS   vi

PREFACE   xi

1 BEFORE THE STORM – POLITICAL ISSUES PRE-1912   1

2 HOME RULE 1912–14   22

3 IRELAND AND THE FIRST WORLD WAR   49

4 THE EASTER RISING   62

5 THE RISE OF SINN FÉIN 1916–19   76

6 VIOLENCE 1919–23   91

7 NORTHERN IRELAND   107

8 SOUTHERN IRELAND 1923–ONWARDS   125

9 COMMEMORATING OUR PAST 1690–1916   140

REVIEW   156

CONCLUSION   166

APPENDICES
Appendix 1: Artists   173
Appendix 2: Photographers   178
Appendix 3: Valuation of postcards   179

BIBLIOGRAPHY   181

INDEX   184

LIST OF ILLUSTRATIONS

1.1 Independence demonstration
1.2 Hurling sticks
1.3 No justice there
1.4 The land question solved
1.5 In the old days
1.6 Alas! My poor brother
1.7 Irish anti-national exhibition 1907
1.8 The unemployed in Ireland
1.9 Belfast strike – motor vans delivering goods
1.10 Belfast strike – traction engine with goods
1.11 Belfast strike – maxim gun section
1.12 Belfast strike – lorries of paper overturned
1.13 Belfast strike – labour leaders
1.14 Belfast strike – funeral of victims
1.15 Belfast strike – funeral of Charles McMullan and Margaret Lennon
1.16 In memory of Thomas H. Sloan

2.1 Home Rule souvenir (Redmond) and concertina
2.2 We won't have Home Rule and concertina
2.3 Irish national volunteers
2.4 Bravo! Ulster volunteers (marching)
2.5 'For God and Ulster' and message written on reverse
2.6 'C' company Y.C.V.I.
2.7 Y.C.V.I. On parade
2.8 Gough the brave
2.9 Frederick Crawford
2.10 Gun running at Bangor
2.11 Bravo Ulster volunteers (gun runners on the road to Belfast)
2.12 'Fanny'
2.13 No Home Rule
2.14 How is freedom measured?
2.15 Who said Home Rule
2.16 The Home Rule rout
2.17 Tax collector John
2.18 Donegall Place Belfast under Home Rule
2.19 Carrickfergus Castle under Home Rule
2.20 Belfast under Home Rule
2.21 Ulster's prayer don't let go!
2.22 Where are ye drivin' him to, Johnny?
2.23 Intreat me not to leave thee
2.24 Home Rule demonstration Dublin
2.25 Ireland sings her old songs
2.26 Erin sings her old songs

2.27   Home Rule (Erin and Britannia hands across the sea)
2.28   Home Rule (maiden and hound)
2.29   Cat 'We shall begin to look up now!'
2.30   An act of union which satisfies both parties
2.31   Home Rule (husband punched)
2.32   Paddy under Home Rule
2.33   Prehistoric politics

3.1   'The day'
3.2   'Shure he thought we were traitors'
3.3   Irish national volunteers (across the gulf of time)
3.4   Two minds with but a single thought – now!
3.5   Begorra, but ye thocht oi was going to be a thraithor
3.6   Begorra, and he thocht to catch me bending
3.7   With compliments from the Irish brigade to the Prussian Guard
3.8   Charge of the Ulster division
3.9   An Ulster volunteer from Belfast
3.10   The compliments of the season
3.11   Mobilising an Irish conscript
3.12   Drilling an Irish conscript
3.13   Gentle D.O.R.A.
3.14   'Put these on like a good little boy'
3.15   The promised land
3.16   Up Plunkett!

4.1   Sinn Féiners parading
4.2   Armoured motor car
4.3   Searching a hay-cart for rebels or ammunition
4.4 to 4.9   Damage after the rising
4.10   Irish war news
4.11   The burning of Sackville Street Dublin
4.12   Surrender of P.H. Pearse
4.13   Arrest of Edmund Kent
4.14   Cornelius Colbert
4.15   Thomas Ashe
4.16   The fight at Ashbourne
4.17   Friends visiting Sinn Féin prisoners
4.18   Thomas Ashe funeral
4.19   No rest for 'that brute Maxwell!'
4.20   Let Erin remember 1916

5.1   The people's rights
5.2   Making a clean sweep of it
5.3   'Run away home to your foster-mother Johnny'

5.4   'Like all scabs Redmond'
5.5   Shade of Wolfe Tone
5.6   The party 'on the rocks'
5.7   Tom Ashe September 25th, 1917
5.8   The last of the snakes
5.9   Unconquerable
5.10 'Think of the "pawty", John'
5.11 Following in Father's footsteps
5.12 Irish party's French mission 1915
5.13 If
5.14 Arthur Griffith T.D.
5.15 Míceál O Flannagáin, Márta 1919
5.16 'I just want the same full measure'

6.1   1919 house of commons during an Irish debate
6.2   Dáil Éireann an chead tionol
6.3   Dáil Éireann an tarna tionol
6.4   Bobby Byrne funeral
6.5   'Steam is off, black and tan'
6.6   Thomas MacSwiney (memorial)
6.7   Thomas Whelan before execution
6.8   John Doyle (memorial)
6.9   Don't argue shoot!
6.10 Irish peace conference July 1921 – gathering at the mansion house
6.11 Irish peace conference July 1921 – General Macready
6.12 Irish peace conference July1921 – delegation from Irish cities
6.13 The gun to win the day
6.14 Military operations Dublin June–July 1922 – shell exploding on four courts
6.15 Military operations Dublin June–July 1922 – national army reserves at barricade
6.16 Military operations Dublin June–July 1922 – national troops searching civilians
6.17 Military operations Dublin June–July 1922 – national forces bombing Hammam hotel
6.18 Siege of Limerick July 1922 – breach made in strand barracks by artillery
6.19 Funeral of the late General Collins

7.1   Sir James Craig, his son and Lt.-Col. Spender (opening of Northern Ireland parliament)
7.2   Joe's last call
7.3   Mr Joseph Devlin M.P. – the people's friend
7.4   'Toby'
7.5   'It's a little souvenir I bought from Dublin dear'
7.6   'Would you buy a used car from these men?'
7.7   'Returning the empties'
7.8   'Afternoon class in motor maintenance'
7.9   'Tourist information'

7.10 'Provo patrol' revolutionary greetings from Ireland
7.11 'Rubber bullets' chalked body outline
7.12 Dutch demonstration
7.13 Maggie, arretez le massacre, svp!!!
7.14 Bobby Sands
7.15 Long Kesh 1981 'pieta' (mural)
7.16 Mickey Devine
7.17 Miami showband and collusion
7.18 Who will defend Ulster now? (mural)
7.19 Cemented with love (mural)
7.20 Siege of Derry (mural)
7.21 No thoroughfare!
7.22 Sir Edward Carson (plus slogan)
7.23 No Home Rule – united we stand
7.24 No surrender (mural)

8.1 The late Kevin O'Higgins
8.2 Dunne and O'Sullivan memorial
8.3 Beannacht na féile Pádraig (anti-partition)
8.4 Free the Murrays now!
8.5 Shannon electricity scheme
8.6 Eucharistic congress 1932
8.7 'My heart's in dear old Ireland'
8.8 Valentia bridge
8.9 Women's rights
8.10 Travellers' rights
8.11 The Ballygombeen bequest
8.12 Holidays in the sun
8.13 Greetings from Reaganland
8.14 Tell us the truth
8.15 Tony, look me in the eye and tell me I'm safe
8.16 Greetings from Ireland (and reverse)
8.17 United Nations 1945–1995

9.1 Shutting the gates of Derry by the immortal Apprentice Boys
9.2 William's landing at Carrickfergus
9.3 Battle of the Boyne
9.4 Flight of James from Kinsale
9.5 Lady O'Neill
9.6 Edmund Burke M.P.
9.7 Lord Edward Fitzgerald
9.8 The brothers John and Henry Sheares
9.9 The battle of Antrim
9.10 The battle of Ballynahinch
9.11 Lord Castlereagh

9.12   Thomas Russell
9.13   Robert Emmett delivering his famous speech from the dock
9.14   Daniel O'Connell
9.15   Thomas Francis Meagher
9.16   Michael Davitt (museum)
9.17   Padraic Pearse
9.18   James Connolly
9.19   Countess Markievicz

Conclusion
Conclusion 1 Who said we're to have Home Rule?
Conclusion 2 Catapulter
Conclusion 3 Child with 'gun' (Spengler)
Conclusion 4 LPOW and Cúchulainn (mural)
Conclusion 5 Cúchulainn and republican memorial (mural)
Conclusion 6 Cúchulainn Cróga and map of Irish provinces (mural)
Conclusion 7 Drumcree (mural)
Conclusion 8 Vote 'yes'
Conclusion 9 Playboard appeal

Covers
Londonderry under Home Rule
Home Rule 'Shipwreck'
Dr Sinn Féin – Forcible Feeding

PREFACE

The exact origin of the picture postcard is in dispute, but all who have taken an interest in the topic would be in agreement that they date from the latter part of the nineteenth century. What would also be beyond dispute is the era in which they first flourished in Britain and Ireland. That phenomenon can largely be attributed to a decision of the Post Office in 1894, that henceforth, it would accept for delivery cards with pictures. Prior to this, plain cards only, had been accepted by the postal authorities.

Even the plain cards had already proved their popularity, for in their first year of production (1870–71), sales figures had reached 75,000,000. The introduction of pictures further stimulated demand, and yet a further surge was brought about by an Act of Parliament in 1902, which for a charge of a ½d (halfpenny), allowed the sender to include both the address and a message on the reverse, thus leaving the whole of the front available for a picture. This new concession helped usher in a golden age of postcards, which lasted for about a quarter of a century. At the peak of their popularity, about 800,000,000 postcards were being posted per year. (See further "On Postcards" in Bibliography.)

It is not a great exaggeration to claim that the postcard became the internet of its age and more. It combined the roles of post, e-mail, text messaging, travel guide and newspaper photograph. In 1907, the journalist James Douglas called it 'the best guide to the spirit of the Edwardian era', and he justified his claim thus,

> For the picture postcard is a candid revelation of our pursuits and pastimes, our customs and costumes, our morals and manners. … The picture postcard enables the most indolent man to explore the wilds of Switzerland or Margate without perturbation.

Given the popularity of the medium, it is hardly surprising that the picture postcard would also reflect the political issues of the times. This book will focus on the presentation of Irish politics in postcards, and try to present them in their historical context. Some of these cards are fairly well-known, but many of the remainder are rare and will be unfamiliar to all but a very few. It will be argued that often these cards both reflect contemporary opinion and try to influence it. It will seek to display them with comment and explanation, rather than use them, as has been done occasionally in the past, as mere passing illustrations in a detailed historical account. Although the work is not designed primarily as a piece of original historical research, it is hoped that it will be of interest to all those who have a curiosity about our past.

Sean Moran [in an essay in *Images, Icons and the Irish Nationalist Imagination*] provocatively attributes the relative lack of interest amongst historians in images as an historical source, and that would include nearly all the postcards featured here, to their 'fetish' for documentary evidence. Historians conventionally seek 'the facts' and are none too comfortable with the political image, which often distorts those facts, courts the myth, and seeks to appeal to the emotions of the viewer, as much or even more than the intellect. As he says, '… images, as non-textual a kind of evidence as is possible, remain problematic for historians: the content of images is open to endless debate, its influence is seemingly indeterminate, and the non-rational effect images have upon people is mysterious' (Mc Bride, *Images, Icons and the Irish Nationalist Imagination*). This book will not attempt to devalue the conventional textual approach, but it will seek to increase understanding by also highlighting the power of the image.

Those who read this work will have some interest in Irish history. It is assumed they will have some knowledge, at least of the broad outline of major events. Consequently, the short introductory essay to each chapter will not seek to go into a detailed narrative. Instead, it will seek to do two things. First it will indicate the range of postcards covering a topic. Secondly, it will then sketch some details of events as shown in the postcard range. Within each chapter the chosen samples will be described in greater detail, recognising their strengths and limitations.

Nobody knows yet how many cards on an Irish political theme have been produced, but only a tiny fraction of those issued can be displayed in a single book. It is hoped that this representative selection will prove sufficient to portray a wide range of political opinion, including the views of the constitutional nationalist, the republican, the unionist, the British and the largely uncommitted observer. Throughout the commentaries, an earnest attempt has been made to avoid bias, although that verges upon the impossible in relation to the controversial events of Irish history.

BEFORE THE STORM
POLITICAL ISSUES PRE-1912

Introduction

The decade or so before the third Home Rule crisis of 1912 may appear comparatively dull and unimportant when set beside the political maelstrom of the following years. Neither threat of sedition nor mass political movements, neither rebellion nor civil war dominated the picture, in contrast to the years 1912–23.

Nevertheless, this was far from being a featureless period. Although they may lack some of the dramatic impact of the latter years, significant events of these years were recorded on postcards for posterity. These preserve and present, for example, evidence of Irish attitudes to enlistment in the British Army, of an attempt to square the Irish political circle with a form of devolution acceptable to unionists and nationalists, of advanced nationalism in the form of Sinn Féin propaganda from the Dungannon Clubs, and even of an early Irish independence campaign, at a time when that particular movement was at a very low ebb.

They include also a jocular reference to the Irish land question, to the theft of the 'Irish Crown Jewels', the Dublin International Exhibition of 1907 viewed from one particular political viewpoint, and a comprehensive pictorial record for the Belfast strike of the same year, which arose from the upsurge of working class politics, and in its turn helped to exacerbate tensions within unionism. More than half the cards available in this early period deal with that particular dispute.

Some of the issues highlighted in these early cards, such as the land question, looked more to the past. Nevertheless, others such as union recognition and even more so, the constitutional question, abstentionism and resistance to enlistment in the British military were again to be of major importance in the future. Although there is a certain degree of linkage between most of these topics each has been treated independently within this chapter.

* * * * *

Cultural rather than political nationalism was a more prominent feature in Ireland around 1900. Movements like the GAA and the Gaelic League were gaining in strength, while the campaign for political separation from Britain, most recently represented by the Fenian movement, was now little more than a vague historical memory, despite the survival, mostly in exile of leading figures like John Devoy, Thomas Clarke, Jeremiah O'Donovan Rossa and John O Leary.

Even the Home Rule movement was in the doldrums. After the split in the Home Rule party, the downfall of Parnell (1890), and the defeat of the second Home Rule bill in 1893, constitutional nationalism too seemed to have little prospect of success.

Despite this, there were groups, such as the rump of the IRB, Griffith and Rooney's Cumann na nGaedheal, and for women, Inghinidhe na hÉireann, along with the Dungannon Clubs, founded soon after in 1905, and individuals like the journalist Denis Moran of *The Leader*, who actively campaigned for Irish political and economic independence. An anonymous organisation or individual of this political persuasion was undoubtedly responsible for advertising an independence demonstration at Beresford Place, in front of Dublin's Custom House.

1.1

This card (no. 1.1) and the rally, which it advertises cannot be dated with certainty, but there is an indication that the card is pre-1902 in origin, as it does not carry the horizontal dividing line on the back, which is a mark of post-1902 cards. The only known producer of Irish political postcards at that time was the Dungannon Club in Belfast, but its earliest known productions were not published until 1906–07.

At least two major political demonstrations in Beresford Place during this period can be easily identified. The first of these was organised by the Dublin Transvaal Committee, a body supported by the United Irish League and both constitutional and revolutionary nationalists. Its prime aim was to oppose the Boer War, 1899–1902, and in particular the recruitment of Irishmen into the British Army.

A later meeting took place here in June 1911 to oppose any formal address of welcome to King George V on his visit to Dublin. Opposition to the Royal visit was co-ordinated by the United National Societies Committee. 'The O Rahilly,' who was secretary to this somewhat obscure committee, erected a banner across

Grafton Street bearing the slogan, 'Thou art not conquered yet, dear land'. Needless to say, the authorities could not tolerate such a sentiment on the route of the Royal procession, and it was promptly removed by the Dublin Metropolitan Police. On balance it seems more likely that the latter was the context for this postcard rather than the Boer War.

The artwork of the card is far from being memorable and the main message is nothing out of the ordinary. Of course it does not need to be as it is purely functional, being an advertisement for a political demonstration. Advertising was a common function of postcards at the time. The most interesting feature of the card is the Gaelic slogan on the banner: '*Múscail do mhisneach a Bhanba*', which, given a rather liberal translation here, might be more literally rendered as, 'Ireland, awaken your courage.' The general purpose of the advertised demonstration would appear to be to raise the drooping spirits of dispirited nationalists.

The Gaelic line has been borrowed from a well-known seventeenth century poem of the Dominican priest, Padraigín Haicéad, a work which he wrote *c.* 1646 during a particularly turbulent era in both Irish and British history.

In England, the Civil War had been in progress since 1642. In Ireland, the Confederation of Kilkenny had been formed, mainly to further the interests of the Anglo-Irish (Old English) Catholics. Haicead maintained a regular correspondence with Rinuccini, the nuncio dispatched by the Pope to liaise with the Confederation. This body was supposed to unite the native Irish and Old English Catholics, but failed to do so. That is hardly surprising since the Confederation itself was frequently torn apart by internal dissensions.

Although the native Irish leader, Owen Roe O Neill, won a famous victory at Benburb in 1646, disaster was on the horizon for many Irish Catholics. With the arrival of Cromwell in 1649, their fortunes were soon brought to a sorry state, most

1.2

No Justice There.

1.3

notably after the sieges of Drogheda in September and Wexford the following month. However, if Ireland could survive this its darkest hour, then, as the card acclaims, there was no need for current despair.

The use of the Gaelic quotation on this card would fit in well with the linguistic revival being promoted since 1893 by the Gaelic League, and the drawing of inspiration from past history, whether in pictorial or written form, was to be a pretty constant feature in postcards of the future, as it had been in many cartoons in the latter part of the Victorian era.

Another unusual early card, (no. 1.2) a very rare hand-painted curio, postmarked August 1907, creates or at least stresses the developing association between the Irish sporting, linguistic and political. In its rather crudely painted vignette, it brings together the political and linguistic 'Sinn Féin', with the traditional harp and shamrock of Ireland, and the hurling symbols of the Gaelic Athletic Association (GAA). While it does not add anything much to our understanding, it highlights some contemporary relationships which were to be of growing importance.

A further very early example of an Irish postcard (no. 1.3) on a political theme, this sample bearing a postmark for 24 August 1906, is most probably similar in its origin to the two previous cards. Clearly it is criticising the British judicial system in Ireland, although no detailed or specific grounds are put forward to support this sweeping criticism.

Modern readers, unless they are familiar with postcards during the golden age, may find it surprising to see cards made of peat-moss, but they were a common enough feature of this time without necessarily being used to promote any political agenda. They were but one of the numerous gimmicks employed by manufacturers of postcards to maximise sales. Irish peat-moss was turned into a suitable format for postcards of varying sorts, mainly non-political it has to be said, at a mill in Celbridge, County Kildare.

Nevertheless, the caption, the trademark promoting Irish industry, and the use of peat-moss do appear politically motivated in this case. Contemporary separatists propounded Irish self-sufficiency. It is sometimes forgotten that the original Sinn Féin, founded in 1905, did not seek political independence from Britain. Rather it demanded political and economic equality for Ireland under the Crown in the form of a dual monarchy. Protection in the shape of tariffs was demanded to foster Irish industry. Likewise the Dungannon Clubs, contained in their constitution the aim of developing Ireland 'by the exclusive use of Irish manufactures and produce …'.

If or when the government did not respond favourably to these demands, Sinn Féin's proposed strategy was a boycott of Westminster and of British institutions such as the courts. In 1920, during the later War of Independence, Sinn Féin, in keeping with this longstanding policy, established a court system of its own to subvert British authority.

THE LAND QUESTION SOLVED.
LAND-AGENT—"Look here, Gallagher, I'm going to raise your rent next gale."
TENANT—"Bedad, I'm glad to hear it, for I was thinkin' how on earth I was to raise it meself."

1.4

The land question was one of the gravest problems of eighteenth and nineteenth Irish society. Gladstone, in particular, had responded to Irish pressure and had passed a number of Land Acts from 1870 onwards to ameliorate if not quite eliminate Irish tenant grievances. One of those, which remained was referred to in light-hearted fashion by at least one early twentieth-century card (no. 1.4).

Rent was due twice a year on the gale day. Failure to pay left the tenant liable to eviction. Peasants for the most part had been in a very vulnerable position, as up to the final decades of the century, only about a quarter had the security of a lease. By the time this card was issued (postmarked 1907) the problem was near to solution.

As a result of the various Land Acts, the most recent being the Wyndham Act of 1903, many tenants were now in the process of purchasing their own holdings with the help of mortgages funded by the government. Under the latter Act, about seven million acres of land passed into tenant ownership.

Maybe it was this changing climate, which made the topic appropriate as a subject of humour. It certainly could not have been so lightly treated even a quarter of a century earlier. Nevertheless, the ownership of land remained of crucial importance, and it was still an issue capable of creating considerable heat. That fact was underlined in a newspaper article of 07 May 1907. Under the rather sensationalist

1.5

IN THE OLD DAYS.

" I do not think that any Irish Bishop need have any grave apprehension on account of the irreligious blackguardism which any Irish Clemenceau may attempt to bring to bear against him. . . . As far as I can judge, the Irish Party have nothing behind them. They represent no opinion—Catholic or Irish—but are the puppets of the English Liberals in this matter."

—*Extract from the Bishop of Limerick's Letter to the " Freeman's Journal,"* 15th December, 1906.

headline, 'The Land War in The West', the *Belfast Newsletter* reported on United Irish League demonstrations in County Roscommon, 'At night crowds assemble accompanied by bands, and parade along the farms for the purpose of intimidating the owners and occupiers and compelling them to surrender and sell their farms.'

The breakthrough in more or less solving the land problem had come about largely as a result of the 1902 Land Conference of landlords and nationalist politicians,

whose main recommendations were incorporated into Wyndham's Act. Encouraged by this success, some of those involved in the earlier conference believed that constitutional problems could also be tackled in a similar fashion. In 1904 they reorganised themselves as the Irish Reform Association and brought forward proposals for Irish Devolution, as a compromise between the unionists and Home Rulers. Their proposals got nowhere and Ulster unionists, alarmed by the whole idea, went on to form the Ulster Unionist Council in the following year.

However, the idea of some sort of devolution for Ireland was revived after the Liberals came to power in 1906. Although it is not instantly obvious, it is to this renewed set of proposals that card 1.5 refers. When these were put forward, they were not rejected out of hand by Redmond, but one in particular alarmed the Irish bishops, who saw education being withdrawn from church control. Here we have allusion to two important recurring themes in Irish history over the best part of the last two centuries, namely control of education and the influence of the (Roman) Catholic hierarchy. Note the Education Bill which lies at the bishop's feet. Note also the (Irish) Christian Brothers school which sits roofless and derelict, as a forecast result, no doubt, of the proposed legislation.

The selection of the Christian Brothers school was an especially apt image. The Brothers had formed the backbone of Catholic education for all but a minority of wealthy Catholics since the foundation of their Order in 1802. They had resisted all pressure to cooperate with the National School system in Ireland, and were strongly identified at this time with both Irish nationalism and the Irish language. These are the sort of people Redmond was allegedly prepared to sacrifice. This is the sort of threat to Irish identity he seems willing to condone! His policy led to the hypercritical letter from Bishop O Dwyer of Limerick to the *Freeman's Journal*, from which the quotation on the card has been taken, represented here also, as the proverbial 'belt of the crozier.'

The references to Clemenceau, with whom Redmond and his followers are identified here, were to the radical French politician, who had become premier in 1906. Although he was not personally responsible, he was seen as typifying church-state conflict. The history of the Third French Republic had been marked by anti-clericalism, which came to a head early in the twentieth century. In 1901, the Association Law had banned all religious communities, which existed without specific authorisation from the government. In 1905, the government went further in passing the Law of Separation, which not only withdrew state recognition of the church, but also effectively took all church property, including schools under state control.

In any case, although the Irish Council Bill was drafted in 1907, and had its first reading in parliament, it was quickly abandoned. The Ulster Unionists did not need the Irish Council Bill to convince them that Home Rule was Rome Rule, but they could have pointed to the letter quoted here, and the withdrawal of the bill as one bit of additional evidence to support their belief. More advanced Irish nationalists would no doubt, whatsoever, be only too glad to dub the Irish Parliamentary Party as 'puppets of the English Liberals.' However, their day had not yet arrived, although as we shall see later, advanced nationalists themselves were only too glad to pose as defenders of religion in contrast to the Redmondites.

Devolution proved a step too far for unionists, a step too few for Redmondites, eventually, and for the more extreme advanced nationalists a subject of satire, as shown particularly in one of the Dungannon Clubs' cards *Devolution Pie.* Another contemporary card, this one a Belfast unionist production, depicting what appear to be 'Devolution' and 'Home Rule' biscuits, makes its point concisely with the most terse and unambiguous caption 'We want neither.' The three-cornered political struggle here between Redmondites, radical nationalists and unionists was a minor dry run for more important conflicts to come. Soon however, there was a more interesting topic to engage the Irish public.

Sex, religion, politics, royalty and crime are the best of ingredients for a first class story, as the popular press has long since discovered. All were represented in some shape or form in 'Alas! My poor Brother' (no. 1.6). A contemporary would have instantly understood the references in this card, but time has taken its toll, making it unintelligible for most modern viewers, who do not already know the background. It relates to probably the greatest scandal of the age, to the theft of the 'Irish Crown Jewels' from an unlocked and undamaged safe at Dublin Castle in July 1907.

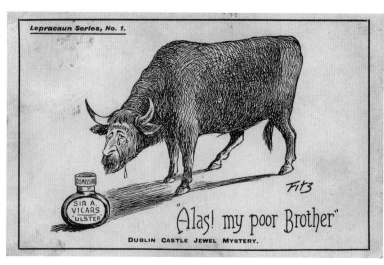

1.6

Sir Arthur Vicars, Ulster King of Arms, had several responsibilities. His chief tasks were to decide questions regarding Irish heraldry, and to advise the Lord Lieutenant of Ireland on all matters of protocol. However, he had an additional, and one would have thought, not very onerous duty, which was to be the keeper of the insignia of the Order of Saint Patrick. These were jewels, which had been presented to the Most Illustrious Order of Saint Patrick by King William IV in 1830, after their discreet recovery by the Crown from an intimate lady friend of his late brother, George IV.

Subsequent investigations into the mysterious theft, involving both Scotland Yard and a Vice-regal Commission of Inquiry, revealed security lapses as well as some lurid details of their guardian's private life. Vicars shared a house with one of his staff, who was revealed as having strong homosexual associations. It is impossible to prove that this had a bearing on Vicars' subsequent dismissal, apparently on the direct orders of King Edward VII, although there is the strongest suspicion that it had. In the King's eyes, all peccadilloes had to be of a heterosexual nature – perhaps?

O'Mahony, shown in the postcard as a bull, was Pierce Gun Mahony (senior), a stepbrother of Vicars. To call the former a colourful character would be a considerable understatement. As a pro-Home Rule MP for the constituency of North Meath, he was one of a minority in his party who had continued supporting Parnell at the time of the split over the Kitty O'Shea case. Loyalty to his leader cost O'Mahony his seat in 1892, when he was defeated by Michael Davitt of Land League fame, who had stood on an anti-Parnell ticket.

In the first decade of the twentieth century, Mahony became a champion of the Bulgarians, who had recently sought and achieved independence from their Turkish masters. Although continuing as a communicant of the Church of Ireland, Mahony was so influenced by his Balkan protégés that he converted to their religion, becoming a member of the Orthodox Church. When a later Church of Ireland minister objected to this cosy ecumenism, Mahony, in protest, converted to Roman Catholicism!

These then are the two main characters depicted in this card. Although O'Mahony (the 'O' comes from his Irish title inherited in 1912) often showed himself both dogged and aggressive in his political campaigning in general and in the pursuit of justice in this case in particular, why he should have been represented as a bull initially seemed a bit of a mystery in itself. Undoubtedly, the humour is rather laboured. The jar labelled, 'Sir A. Vicars. Ulster,' looks remarkably like a Bovril container. By the late nineteenth century this product had already become exceedingly popular. A fine piece of beef (Vicars) appears to have been reduced to a meat extract! This impression is confirmed by the caption, which was a particularly popular contemporary advertising slogan.

No-one has seriously argued that Arthur Vicars himself stole the jewels. Notwithstanding the fact that inquiries after the crime did not show his behaviour to be beyond reproach, Vicars certainly saw himself as a scapegoat, who was treated unfairly following the theft.

Despite his marked difference of political opinion with Vicars, a unionist, O'Mahony campaigned intensively on his stepbrother's behalf following his dismissal. His sympathy is indicated in the caption, 'Alas! My poor Brother.' Vicars did not regain his post, however, and the jewels were never recovered. Even the offer of a substantial reward, £1,000, proved ineffective. A conservative estimate, based on Bank of England figures, would equate this to a present figure in the region of £40,000. The real value of the missing jewels of course, bearing in mind their provenance, is incalculable.

There have been a number of theories, several articles and books, and even a television documentary, all with their own ideas about the culprit or culprits. Some of these suggest a range of political motives and would have implicated Irish republicans, unionists, Lord Aberdeen, the Irish Lord Lieutenant, or even the Royal family. However, theories they all remain, and no-one has ever been made amenable for the crime.

In a dramatic and tragic postscript to these events, the Mahony family home at Kilmorna, near Listowel in County Kerry, was burned down by the IRA during 1921, and the doubly unfortunate Vicars, who was living there at the time, was shot dead.

The theft of the Crown Jewels was the talking-point of the times, but it was not the only excitement that year. The Irish International Exhibition of 1907, which ran from May to November, was a more popular subject for postcard production, although initially these were of the souvenir type rather than the political.

This was to be the largest exhibition of its type ever held in the country. Throughout its six months' existence, the event attracted large crowds from all over

Ireland, many of them ferried to Dublin by special excursion trains. On 24 June, for example, the *Irish Times* reported that 'nearly two thousand employees' came from Gallaher's in Belfast. Official representation from France, Italy, New Zealand, Canada and 'a party of tidy little Japs' contributed to what the same paper called 'the worldwide character of the gathering.' King Edward VII considered it sufficiently important to merit a Royal visit, during which, it was also originally intended, that he should conduct an investiture for the Order of Saint Patrick, using the 'Irish Crown Jewels' referred to previously.

For their entrance fee, the hefty sum of 5 shillings, later reduced to one, visitors were treated to a display of their wares by hundreds of firms from throughout Ireland in what was called the Home Industries Section. In the Fine Arts galleries, there was an extensive display of British, Irish and foreign oil paintings, included works by Millais, Rossetti, Corot and Millet.

Additional attractions, many of which were not covered by the basic entrance fee, included a 'Machinery in Motion' demonstration, a 'Great Water Chute', a 'Switchback railway', a 'Helter Skelter', 'Indian Theatre', a 'Somali village', a 'Crystal Maze', 'Bees', 'Ants' and 'Rivers of Ireland', Cinematographic, Music and Fireworks displays. Many of these were depicted separately in postcards.

A modern Irish reader may find the existence of a vegetarian restaurant in 1907 mildly surprising as such establishments might be considered a modern phenomenon. Not so surprising to some would be the reaction to the limited Sunday opening introduced from 02 June. Amongst several complaints, one letter to the press railed against 'Sabbath desecration.'

All in all, this Exhibition was clearly a major social event, although the superlatives lavished upon it by the *Irish Times* should be treated with a touch of scepticism.

> In the magnitude of its design, the perfection of its detail, the extent, quality and character of its contents, the Exhibition of 1907 reveals not only a marvellous vision of industrial and art development unimagined a quarter of a century ago, but provides us with the equally unmistakable evidence and promises that a commercial and social future, brighter than perhaps even now is dreamt of, lies within the grasp of the country.

Others saw it as being much more than just a social event, and were far from being as impressed as 'The *Irish Times* Correspondent.' *The Republic*, a newspaper published in Belfast as the organ of the Dungannon Club, saw the Exhibition in economic and political terms as detrimental to Irish interests, and was scathingly critical in this poster, subsequently offered for sale in postcard form as part of its Republican Series (no. 1.7).

Poster for an impending Exhibition without apologies to anyone.

Resentment at economic domination of Ireland by Britain had a long history, including the writings of Dean Swift and the later College Green demonstration of the Irish Volunteers with their placarded canons , 'Free Trade or This', to name but two, but again it appears to have been the Dungannon Clubs who first highlighted it in a twentieth-century postcard (1.7).

Here a bedraggled hag oversees a cascade of goods for the Dublin 'Anti-National Exhibition.' She could represent a dominant Britannia astride Ireland, but is more likely to be Erin or Hibernia harassed by a plethora of salesmen. The Irish are to be conned with 'soft soap', and will be bombarded with other produce, 'not good enough for the English market', 'Made In England Which Is Near Ireland', and yet more of the same '*Deanta I Sasana*' (Gaelic, which a majority would not understand, and as a result be more easily fooled, for 'Made in England') and 'Rubbish From The Orient.' As a final flourish, and the ultimate insult to nationalist sensitivities, the cartoonist has shown her bearing that most Irish of instruments, the traditional Irish harp with a figurehead who can only represent England.

In one of three articles criticising the Exhibition, this separatist paper quoted with approval the resolution passed by the Federated Societies of Liverpool. The cartoon would lead one to the same conclusion as the article except that the image conveys its message, maybe not with more force, but certainly without ambiguity and with a little more finesse.

> That in as much as we believe the Dublin International Exhibition, 1907, has been conceived in the interests of Irish place-seekers and foreign manufacturers, and in opposition to the present industrial revival, we call upon all Irish people in Ireland and abroad to abstain from supporting the said exhibition (*The Republic*, 07 Feb. 1907).

All this was three months before it even opened! A slightly different more overt and even more strident anti-British stance was taken in one of its later articles shortly after the opening.

On the opening day it was a demonstration in force to advertise the British Army, with a Viceregal procession so wickedly bungled that it would serve for a burlesque on a state pageant; and on the following Monday the British Navy was enthroned. If there had been any doubt as to the real nature of this enterprise that masquerades as Irish this glorification of the forces against which every honest Irishman is arrayed would have served to damn it out of hand (ibid, 16 May 1907).

One cannot help observing that in a different era, the signature P. O'Neill (the mythical signatory of IRA statements) would not look out of place here!

John Killen, in his *John Bull's Famous Circus – Ulster History through the Postcard 1905–1985*, identified a dozen cards in the republican series from the same source as no. 7. One other in the range condemned the economic domination of Ireland from England and promoted Sinn Féin as the only effective opposition to it. Others were critical of the Irish Parliamentary Party's attendance at Westminster, of the crumbs of Devolution proposed for Ireland, of British Imperialism in general and of recruitment in Ireland for the British Army ('Catching Recruits' – a postcard published for the Dungannon Club).

THE UNEMPLOYED IN IRELAND.
The Police, having little or no duties to perform, have been lately engaged in removing anti-enlistment bills from the dead walls and telegraph poles.

1.8

Both Irish enlistment in the British Army and opposition to it, have a long history, and have occasioned much political argument. Anti-enlistment propaganda during the Boer War had been coordinated by the likes of Arthur Griffith and Maud Gonne McBride, although not in so far as is known in postcard form. That specific style of protest was introduced a little later by the Dungannon Clubs. As was to be the case later in 1914, Irish involvement in the British Army elicited two very different Irish reactions. Although it is only of marginal interest here, there is a copy of a postcard published by Eason & Son in McCracken's history of the Irish involvement in what was then a recent war, which extols the courage of an Irish soldier (captioned 06 January 1901, 'Private Barry Firing Into The Maxim Gun'). One must strongly suspect that it was intended just as much to encourage further Irish recruitment, setting a precedent for similar propaganda during the First World War.

In addition to those Dungannon Club cards identified by Killen, another caricatures 'The Recruiting Sergeant', while a further example from the same source in the National Library of Ireland, poked fun at the police in their attempts to counter resistance to enlistment (no. 1.8). Its caption, 'The Unemployed in Ireland', and the accompanying explanation leave no need for further description. This theme and the other Irish political issues mentioned above have all been recurring subjects in postcard production. When Irish cartoonists had started a few years previously to counter anti-Irish Victorian propaganda in cartoon form, they highlighted three Irish grievances, namely, the landlords, the courts and the British Army. It can hardly be a coincidence that the same targets come into view in these early twentieth-century postcards.

However, one further observation can be made regarding this particular card. While one is conscious of the need for caution lest too much significance is attributed to the jibe in a single card, it clearly identifies the police with politics and in particular sees them as part of the pro-British establishment in Ireland. There is plenty of evidence elsewhere to confirm such a role for the RIC. This labelling, while not particularly important at this time, was to have dire consequences for the same force little more than a decade later.

Before the opening of the Exhibition in Dublin, worker unrest had broken out in Belfast. The Belfast strikes of 1907 have their own important niche in Irish labour history, but are also significant as a precursor of the 1913 Dublin Lockout which was, itself featured in postcards. The main issue for the strike leadership in both cases, and for at least some of the workers, was union recognition. However, in the Belfast case, the situation was further complicated by unprecedented unrest within the Royal Irish Constabulary (RIC). This whole episode was extensively covered in postcards produced by more than one publisher. It was thought necessary to include slightly more narrative than usual on this affair.

Although it was not the first strike that year, serious trouble first flared in the Belfast docks at the end of April, when a number of coal 'fillers' were locked out by their employers at York Dock. They were members of Jim Larkin's National Union of Dock Labourers. The local press, (*Belfast Newsletter*, 30 April) forecast a general strike of dock-workers within days. In this they were correct.

The employers responded to the general walkout by importing non-Union labour from Liverpool. This infuriated local Union men and the imported workers were often met by stone-throwers.

The *Belfast Newsletter*, investigating the cause of the dispute, came up with a number of different explanations. On 09 May, it reported that some workers blamed, 'the long hours and wages question and others the giving of employment to non-

BELFAST STRIKE.—Motor Vans delivering Goods in the Principal Streets of the City under Police Escorts.

1.9

union men —.' Although mention was made of a wage claim, namely of 6d. per hour for a 60-hour week with 9d. per hour overtime rate, Larkin himself specifically stated that his followers insisted only upon 'the right to organize' (*BNL*, 17 May).

The chairman of the company in dispute, The Belfast Steamship Company, was the tobacco baron, Thomas Gallaher. At one stage, the unrest spilled over into his York Street factory. Following a mass-meeting of the factory girls, at which Larkin spoke, urging them to organise themselves into a trade union, seven girls were dismissed. This precipitated a walkout of about 1,000 others. It was, however, only a diversion from the main action.

It was late in May before the next major escalation occurred. Then the dispute was extended to involve the workers on the Fleetwood, Barrow-in-Furness and Heysham services. Again the dispute was about more than money. The Docker's Union had asked for a rise but the employers 'declined to recognise the right of the union officials to interfere in matters of this kind …' (*BNL*, 17 May).

Carters employed by Messrs Wordie and Co. and Messrs Cowan and Co. next went on strike in sympathy with the dockers, refusing to transport goods to and from the docks. The Carriers Association, representing, the employers followed with an ultimatum that they must return to work, 'or the whole of the carters of Belfast will be locked out —' (*BNL*, 04 July). The coal merchants now entered the fray with a declaration that, 'no person representing any union or combination will receive recognition.' (*BNL*, 12 July). In response all coalmen walked out. A serious shortage of coal soon led to closures and lay-offs amongst the larger industrial concerns of the city.

In response and in near desperation, the employers of the city started to use motor lorries and even a traction engine with police protection, to ferry goods to and from the docks (nos 1.9 and 1.10). All this time, the dockers and their

BELFAST STRIKE.—Traction Engine with Goods Guarded by Police. 1.10

supporters held mass meetings and engaged in 'peaceful picketing' as permitted by the recent (December 1906) Trade Unions and Trade Disputes Act, but there was also sporadic illegal action, when 'blacklegs' were stoned, police escorts were attacked and unprotected carts were overturned, as was also illustrated on a number of cards.

Just when the strikes appeared to be building to a climax, there was both good and bad news. The coal strike, which was having the most obvious effect of all the strikes was settled during the last week of July, but disquieting rumours began to circulate about grievances amongst the Belfast constabulary. The *Belfast Newsletter* launched a scathing attack on the nationalist press for what it dubbed its exaggerated reports. 'It is practically suggested that something like a mutiny has occurred.'

The nationalist press was closer to the truth on this occasion and worse was to come. It was soon to be reported in the *Newsletter*'s own headlines that police were, 'In Revolt', and further that, 'Men Defy Their Officers'. Meetings of disgruntled officers took place in Musgrave Square Barracks in contravention of RIC regulations. Reportedly up to sixty men attended one meeting. The men demanded that their grievances over pay be redressed. One of the more dramatic reports was the unintentionally alarmist declaration in *BNL* on 31 July. It sought to reassure its readership by stating that 'until the end of the week at least, the men will continue to do their duty and obey their officers —!'

The police action was not a direct response to the other strikes, but rather arose from longstanding grievances over the absence of a pay-rise for twenty years, while the cost of living had 'exorbitantly increased' (*BNL*, 29 July). Nevertheless, the strikes had played their part at least as a catalyst as the newspaper stated the following day: 'the extra duties imposed upon the men by reason of the present unhappy labour troubles, undoubtedly brought matters to a crisis —.'

BELFAST STRIKE.—Maxim Gun Section of the Middlesex Regiment in Ormeau Park   1.11

The paper went on to say in the following edition that the police involved argued that their representations would have been ignored, had they deferred action until the labour troubles had ended. They also went so far as to circulate RIC Head Constables and sergeants seeking their support for a strike and agitation 'in order to force the concessions claimed.' (*BNL*, 01 August) The situation was now serious enough to grab the attention of the London press. The *Daily Chronicle* found it 'difficult to imagine any situation more fraught with possibilities of peril than the conjunction of large and perhaps turbulent strikes in the industries of the city with a mutiny of the police …'.

The civil authorities were naturally alarmed by these developments and they rushed troops to Belfast, amongst whom were the Cameron Highlanders, and detachments from the Royal Sussex, Royal Berkshire and Middlesex Regiments. *BNL* reported the arrival of hundreds of troops. The *Irish Times* claimed that as many as 4,000 were sent. Groups of them appear in more than one card and as clearly suggested in this card, they came well prepared for trouble (no. 1.11).

Police 'reinforcements' were also recruited in both Derry and Louth to come to Belfast, while those of dubious loyalty already stationed there, 'said to reach as high as two hundred,' were transferred out of the city. Constable Barrett, the ringleader of the dissidents was dismissed from the force and six others had charges brought against them. It appeared that the crisis had passed, but appearances were misleading as the police dispute had simply distracted attention somewhat from the ongoing problems at the docks.

Just after noon on Saturday 10 August, serious rioting broke out 'unexpectedly, rapidly and fiercely …' (*BNL*), when three flour vans going to the quays were attacked as they left the Model Flour Mills on Divis Street. Rioting persisted for about two hours, but military reinforcements managed to bring the situation under control.

An escalation of trouble on the following day seems to have centred on Leeson Street, about half a mile away. It then spread to Springfield and Grosvenor Roads nearby, leaving 'many seriously injured'.

The trouble continued in the wider Falls district after nightfall on Monday 12 August, resulting in the reading of the Riot Act and the subsequent shooting dead of two Conway Street residents, Charles McMullan and Maggie Lennon, and the wounding of several others.

Strike leaders and local clergy made strenuous efforts to restore peace. In all probability, it was the shock of the deaths more than anything else, which also jolted the strikers and employers into seeking an immediate settlement. There was a partial return to work by the carters before the end of that week, and all had returned by the following Monday.

Although this must have put pressure on the dockers, they remained on strike until September. On returning to work, they received no pay rise though they did attain recognition, Larkin's prime aim, but at a terrible cost.

All major aspects of the strike were featured in a wide range of contemporary postcards. Employers, for example, brought in non-union workers to drive vehicles for them in an attempt to beat the strikers. They were often attacked by mobs and their loads were scattered over the road, subsequently necessitating permanent police protection (no. 1.12). It was probably one of the reasons for the use of the traction engine that its weight would render it less vulnerable to that sort of attack.

To keep up their morale, the strikers met frequently, often on a daily basis. Many of their meetings were addressed by Jim Larkin himself (no. 1.13). The outcome of the most serious violence which left several in hospital and resulted in the two Falls Road fatalities was also recorded (nos 1.14 and 15).

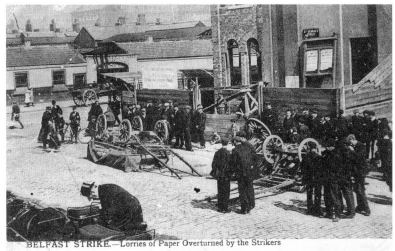

BELFAST STRIKE.—Lorries of Paper Overturned by the Strikers

1.12

BELFAST STRIKE.—Labour Leaders addressing the Strikers at Queen's Square, Belfast
Messrs M'Keown   Boyd   Larkin   Murray   M'Kessock   1.13

In general, the producers of these cards, of whom Waltons and Boyd were the most important, do not seem to editorialise as it were. They simply produced photographs of general public interest. The cards issued by them could be seen as a slideshow, narrating in some detail the main events of the strike. While the intentions of the publishers do not in themselves appear political, there is no denying the cards' political content. Union recognition and workers' rights were major issues in Britain and Ireland from the late nineteenth century.

Some writers have attributed particular political importance to these events of 1907 because they induced workers to cross religious and political boundaries. Certainly Larkin himself claimed that he united workers irrespective of religion. The cross-channel dockers in the York Dock were both Protestant and unionist. They attracted the support of Joe Devlin, nationalist MP for West Belfast, and it was in Catholic West Belfast that the most serious violence occurred. Yet, the unifying force of the strikes is far from conclusively proven. In any case, the unity, if it existed at all, was not clearly illustrated in postcards, and was shown to be very shallow, as was soon to be demonstrated in the conflicts over Home Rule.

Before that, however, there was conflict of a different type within Unionism itself. Nationalists had been severely split in the previous decade, following Parnell's affair with Kitty O'Shea. Unionist divisions were more of a short-term schism, although they had surfaced from time to time in different forms.

In 1902, when the South Belfast parliamentary seat became vacant, Tom Sloan, leader of the Belfast Protestant Association, stood in the by-election, defeating the official Conservative and Unionist candidate.

Although staunch in his Unionism, and hostile to Catholicism, the new MP showed firm support for the growing cause of labour. On his expulsion from the Orange Order, Sloan went on to found the Independent Orange Order. In the 1906

FUNERAL OF
VICTIMS,
BELFAST RIOTS,
AT DUNVILLE
PARK.

J. W. Boyd.

1.14

FUNERAL OF
CHARLES
M'MULLAN AND
MARGARET
LENNON,
VICTIMS OF
BELFAST
RIOTS.

J. W. Boyd

1.15

general election Tom Sloan held his seat. The following year he formed an alliance of sorts with both William Walker, the Labour candidate for North Belfast, and Joe Devlin from West Belfast in supporting the strikers.

By 1910, the more traditional Conservative and Unionist forces had regrouped, and Sloan's political career came to an abrupt end, when he lost his seat. Although the split was of fairly minor importance, card no. 1.16 rather cleverly conveys some of the bitterness which it created.

Reproduced in the form of a memorial card, it gloats on Sloan's political eclipse. The verse is the best part of the card. It is a parody of an extract from the popular nineteenth-century poem, 'The Burial of Sir John Moore at Corunna.'

Moore had been British commander in Portugal. Late in 1808, he led an army into Spain, to support the Spaniards' defence against Napoleon. Although he was forced to retire through the mountains of Galicia to the port of La Coruna on the north-western tip of Spain, he prevented a French attack on southern Spain. The cost for the British was high, and Moore himself was killed, before the British forces were successfully evacuated.

The parody of this poem mimics the style and metre of the original, but the tone in markedly different. The verses composed by Charles Wolfe, a Church of Ireland clergyman, were once familiar to most Irish schoolboys. Wolfe's original lamented the loss of Moore, while the copy on the card rejoiced at the political demise of Sloan. The contrast is obvious when viewing this extract from the original alongside the verses in no.1.16.

We buried him darkly at dead of night,
The sods with our bayonets turning;
By the struggling moonbeam's light
And the lantern dimly burning.

No useless coffin enclosed his breast
Not in sheet or in shroud we wound him
But he lay like a warrior taking his rest
With his martial cloak around him.

Lightly they'll talk of the spirit that's gone
and o'er his cold ashes upraid him,
But little he'll reck, if they let him sleep on
In a grave where a Briton has laid him.

There is at least one other card very similar in format to this. It also takes the form of a memorial card, showing a grave in the 'Political Cemetery', with an inscription, 'IN MEMORY OF SLOAN', and accompanied by a rather laboured verse. Although both cards accurately recorded the political demise of Sloan, he should not be dismissed too lightly as he represented a populist strain in unionism which has persisted.

By 1910 then with their forces regrouped after the defeat of Sloan, the Unionist establishment was more ready to face the threat from the Liberal parliamentary alliance with the forces of nationalist Ireland.

Postcards in this period are much less numerous than those of the next decade, but those which do exist highlight some crucial interlinked political issues. While the representation of each of these has been looked at separately here, the areas of political dispute could coalesce into a coherent political philosophy. At its most simplistic, an Irish nationalist would argue that Britain was the source of all Ireland's ills.

IN MEMORY
OF
Thomas H. Sloan

Late Member of Parliament for South Belfast,

WHO DEPARTED HIS PARLIAMENTARY LIFE

ON THE

20th day of January, 1910,

And was interred in the Home Rule Cemetery.

R.I.P.

(Resurrection Indefinitely Postponed)

Sentenced to Death by Loyal Unionist Electors
of South Belfast, and duly executed by
JAMES CHAMBERS, ESQ., K.C., M.P.

We buried him openly—not at dead of night,
  But at noon, when the poll had been counted ;
When the Sheriff had told us how we'd won the fight
  On our shoulders his body we mounted.

No useless coffin enclosed his breast,
  Nor in sheet, nor in shroud we wound him ;
But he lay like a "wobbler," needing a rest,
  With his fur coat wrapped around him.

Little we'll rack of the member that's gone,
  And o'er his cold ashes weep for him ;
What we'll say is, 'For Heaven's sake let him sleep on,'
  "We'll take jolly good care we won't wake him."

GONE WHENCE HE CAME, WHICH IS FAR BETTER.

1.16

Thus, as has been argued in some of the postcards shown, her economy was blighted by British competition, with Ireland used as a dumping ground for inferior British products. Her farmers struggled to pay excessive rents under the threat of eviction. Her citizens could not get justice from a British court system, and her workers were denied the rights, protection and financial gains which trade union recognition might offer them. Political representation at Westminster offered little of substance for Ireland. The panacea they would recommend for all these problems, of course, would be independence, or failing that at least Home Rule.

2

HOME RULE 1912–14

Introduction

The broad picture of the 1912 Home Rule crisis is too well-known to require more than the briefest outlining here. When Asquith's Liberal government, in alliance with Redmond's Irish Parliamentary Party, introduced the third Irish Home Rule Bill in April, Unionist alarm was soon made manifest. In their Solemn League and Covenant of 1912, Ulster Unionists vowed,

> throughout this our time of threatened calamity to stand by one another in defending for ourselves and our children our cherished position of equal citizenship in the United Kingdom, and in using all means which may be found necessary to defeat the present conspiracy to set up a Home Rule Parliament in Ireland … .

While the Liberal government and its Conservative and Unionist opposition were equally matched in the House of Commons, Redmond had the support of more than eighty Irish MPs, thereby guaranteeing a House of Commons majority for the bill. As a result of the Parliament Act this bill, unlike the previous Home Rule Bill of 1892, could henceforth, be delayed only, and not stopped by the Conservative majority in the Lords.

The strong but ultimately ineffective opposition to the Bill in parliament from both Conservative and Unionist politicians was therefore highly predictable. Having failed to defeat the Home Rule measure by parliamentary means, Ulster Unionists now resorted to extra-parliamentary methods. Their mass protest meetings, the establishment of an 'Ulster provisional government', the organisation of the Ulster Volunteer Force (UVF) in January 1913, and the Larne gun-running of April 1914, have all been thoroughly documented elsewhere, and therefore no more than a skeletal narrative has been included here.

However, many would be a good deal less familiar with the extensive unionist publicity campaign, much of it launched through the medium of political postcards. Most of these were undoubtedly designed to galvanise their own supporters at home, but some were also intended to appeal to public opinion on the British mainland.

Irish nationalists could be excused a certain smugness with regard to Home Rule. After all, its passing seemed inevitable given the arithmetic of the House of Commons and the emasculation of the House of Lords by the 1911 Parliament Act. Nevertheless, Home Rulers, like Unionists, did appreciate, at least to a certain extent, the necessity of promoting their cause. This they also did in part through the production of propaganda postcards (nos. 2.24 to 2.29).

Finally, the issue proved a source of amusement for some commentators, viewing events and developments from the outside. They linked the Home Rule issue in particular to the contemporary campaign for women's rights (nos. 2.31 and 2.32).

The range of postcard material on this particular topic is probably broader than for any other examined. This includes numerous photographs of political marches, rallies and leaders, artists' impressions of events, especially of the 1914 unionist gun-running, some clever political cartoons and excruciatingly poor political verse. Clearly identifiable local photographers and publishers, along with anonymous individuals as well as large international firms all contributed to the grand total, on which no-one as yet can put a precise figure.

* * * * *

The flood of postcard material on the Home Rule crisis would create a difficulty for any writer trying to select a starting-point. However, the depiction of the political leadership seems as appropriate an introduction as any alternative. Rotary Photographic, one of the larger postcard producers, issued, as far as can be ascertained, the only 'Real Photograph' of 'The Principal Members of the Provisional Government of Ulster', but photographs of leading individuals were rather more common.

Numerous contemporary images of both Redmond and Carson in particular, were reproduced. From this range two have been selected, (nos. 2.1 and 2.2), since they display not just the leaders themselves but also offer the additional novelty of concertinas of pictures. These show other important political figures, and incorporate propaganda drawings and verse. Although these items could be posted, it seems probable that they, along with a small number of similar novelties known to exist, were intended more as souvenirs for the purchasers.

In card no. 2.1 Redmond appropriately appears before a sketch of the current Bank of Ireland at College Green in Dublin, which had previously been the site of the Irish parliament until the Act of Union in 1800. If Home Rule now materialised as nationalists expected, then the original building would be an obvious and fitting location for the new parliament, although one cannot help feeling that the anticipation smacked somewhat of crossing the bridge before reaching it!

Carson's image on the banner in no. 2.2 is surrounded by conventional slogans. It is accompanied by drummers, and carried in procession by staunch supporters. Predictably the verse pledges all their support for the Union. Marches and mass meetings in themselves can of course be seen as a form of propaganda. Photographic records, of which there are many, spread the message further.

2.1

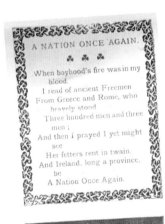

2.2

CAPTAIN J. CRAIG.

COL. WALLACE.

ONE CROWN

ONE PARLIAMENT

HOUSES OF PARLIAMENT.

ONE FLAG

MR BONAR LAW.

LORD LONDONDERRY.

We will not have Home Rule!

" Shall we from the Union sever ?
By the God that made us, NEVER :
Wave the flag we love, for ever
Over us and you. "

Valentine & Sons, Ltd., Dundee and London

It appears th~~ the three different hat styles of the marchers are meant to be indicative of support from different social classes. This interpretation would be supported by an extract from the caption on another card (no. 2.4):

> We are marching, counter-marching, going moonlight on parade,
> From the gentleman of fortune right down through every grade;

By the autumn of 1913, each of these opposing leaders had the backing of a private army (nos. 2.3, 2.4 and 2.5). Although the Irish Volunteers and Ulster Volunteers were never directly committed to fighting each other, the risk of civil war was always a reality. The threat of violence was often merely implied, but here in no. 2.5, it was made most explicit in the words of Earl Spencer.

2.3

2.4

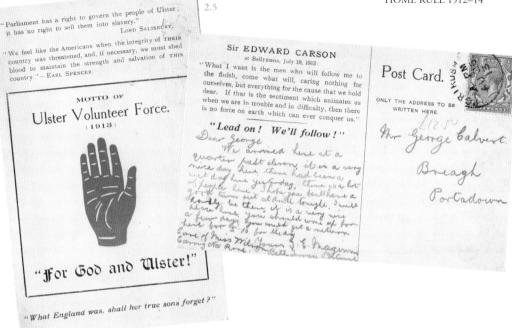

While it is normally the pictures or images created by the artist, which are of prime interest, occasionally the correspondence on a card offers a pleasant bonus. In this particular case (no. 2.5) one Ulster Volunteer writes to a friend and fellow member from his holiday lodgings, referring to the drill session he will miss that night. In all these political dramas, it is worth remembering that we are dealing with real people engaged in mundane, ordinary activities such as buying train tickets and going off to the seaside for a few days.

Anybody with even the most cursory knowledge of these historical events will be aware of the existence of the UVF and Irish Volunteers. Fewer will know of the YCVI or Young Citizens Volunteers of Ireland. Founded in September 1912 in Belfast, they first met in Belfast City Hall under the Presidency of the Lord Mayor. They could be seen as a cross between senior boy scouts and an unofficial Territorial Army unit. These Volunteers were open to young men between the ages of eighteen and thirty-five, and while theoretically non-sectarian, they were in practice, both Protestant and loyalist.

Members paid a 2/6 (half-crown) joining fee, as well as a weekly subscription and had in addition to purchase their own uniforms (bluish-grey with purple facings, silver badges and buttons). At weekly sessions they received training in drill, rifle practice, signalling, knots and, where possible, first aid. It might be noted here in passing how the postcard was used as a reminder of a forthcoming parade, something which might be accomplished in modern times by telephone, e-mail or mobile text message (no. 2.6).

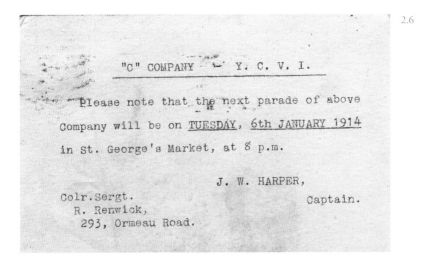

2.6

The YCVI does not seem to have prospered outside Belfast. Possibly its expansion was hindered by the considerable costs of membership. By 1913, when the government refused it recognition as a Territorial Army unit, membership had started to drift away towards the UVF. It was officially subsumed into the larger body in June 1914. This was marked by a march to Balmoral Showgrounds, where it was reviewed alongside the UVF by Sir Edward Carson. This picture (no. 2.7) may very well represent that march.

Although the organisation had by and large disappeared at the time war broke out, a separate identity was still recognised when members were allocated to their own military unit, the 14th Battalion of the Royal Irish Rifles within the 109th Infantry Brigade.

Perhaps these Volunteers have been given a prominence here which is greater than their importance merits, but it is thought justifiable to redress their almost complete omission from other accounts. In so far as a photograph of this sort (no. 2.7) adds to our understanding of unionist activities at this time, it could be argued that pictures showing the YCVI so well turned out in quasi-military uniform lent further evidence to the degree of unionist preparedness to resist Home Rule by all and every means.

In any case, it was neither political threats, nor quasi-military marches, or any of these Volunteers groups, which struck the first crucial blow against Home Rule. Rather it was the event commemorated here in another card. (no. 2.8). At first or even second glance, this particular nondescript postcard hardly seems worthy of comment, but impressions often can be, and in this case certainly are, deceptive.

Beneath the all too predictable crossed flags, the uninspiring verse/song appears of very limited interest. However, it would be a grave mistake to dismiss this so lightly, as it refers to what was arguably, one of the turning points of twentieth-century Irish history.

'Gough the Brave', extolled in the title, was Brigadier General Sir Hubert Gough, 'leader' of the Curragh Mutiny. When Asquith's government introduced the Third Home Rule Bill in parliament, Unionists reacted with a mixture of propaganda, demonstrations and threats, some of which we have already seen. Urged on by the likes of Winston Churchill, Asquith considered the use of force to quash Unionist resistance. As a precaution at least, against possible unionist violence, troops were to be deployed throughout Ulster.

However, before any military action was undertaken, the authorities thought it necessary to clarify the position of Ulstermen amongst the officers. It was decided that they alone would be excused from this duty, but that all others would be required to participate on pain of dismissal. Gough had been born in London and reared in India. Consequently, he did not qualify for an exemption from this operation despite his Ulster connections.

2.8

2.9

In response to the decision taken by General Paget, the Irish Commander-in-Chief, to garrison Ulster, Gough chaired a meeting in March 1914 of fifty-eight officers, not an 'Immortal One Hundred' as claimed. They indicated their intention of resigning their commissions, in preference to participating in the possible coercion of Ulster Unionists.

Amidst confusion, assurances and denials, the government fudged the issue and backed away from confrontation. This was the famous 'Curragh Mutiny', which virtually guaranteed the abandonment of Home Rule, or at the very least the exclusion of Ulster from its terms. Some such outcome became all the more likely, some would say virtually certain, with the resounding success of the Larne gun-running in the following month.

Although in one sense the actions of Gough and the government's reaction were vital as a public manifestation that the army was an 'impotent weapon' (Dutton, p. 229) for the crushing of Ulster Unionist opposition, many political insiders would have reached this conclusion some time before. The War Office, for example, previously had reckoned that up to a third of all army officers would resign rather than coerce the Ulster loyalists, (ibid., p. 223) while Lord Milner was amongst those who wished to make it Conservative party policy that any officers who might resign under these circumstances would be reinstated by a Conservative government (ibid., p. 226). The threat to the Ulster Unionist position may already have passed, though they themselves were not convinced of that.

To ensure that their own threats were more than empty words, and to reinforce their resistance to Home Rule 'using all means which may be found necessary', Unionists now considered it essential to procure a large quantity of arms and ammunition for the UVF. According to A.T.Q. Stewart, Frederick Crawford (shown in sample no. 2.9 wearing his regimental uniform), had been arguing since 1886, that only armed resistance would stop Home Rule, and already in 1913 he had imported several thousand rifles from England.

However, this quantity was insufficient to satisfy the demands of UVF members and Crawford was accordingly given the task by the arms committee of the Ulster

2.10

GUN RUNNING AT BANGOR, CO. DOWN, APRIL 25TH, 1914.

2.11

BRAVO, ULSTER VOLUNTEERS!   The Gun Runners on the road to Belfast from Larne.

Unionist Council of organising a much larger shipment. This of course was the famous Larne gun-running (nos. 2.10 and 2.11).

The fact that a quantity of the shipment was offloaded for landing at Bangor (no.2.10) and Donaghadee is less well-known than the main landing at Larne. One would assume that artists' impressions have been used in these cards partly because much of the activity took place under cover of darkness and this would have posed major, possibly even insuperable, technical difficulties for photographers of the time. Given that the action was highly illegal, a photographer was probably too much of a luxury for an historian to expect and too much of a risk for the organisers to encourage in any case.

Following their triumph in the gun-running, unionists were naturally ecstatic. Police searches for arms drew a blank. This was reflected in a range of postcards in

2.12

There's a smart little steamship named "FANNY,"
Whose movements had been most uncanny,
Her Gun-Running gigantic
Has made Asquith quite frantic—
He'd like to do something, but can he?

the Historic Events Series, which gloated over police and government impotence. Home Rule was effectively on its deathbed. Unionist joy was particularly well represented in this card (no. 2.12), which commemorated the exploits of one of the gun-running boats with this clever limerick accurately expressing the political reality after April 1914.

In addition to these literary efforts, whatever their merits, the artist's brush and cartoonist's pen gave them considerable scope in going beyond the purely narrative, into expressing unionist attitudes, arguments and propaganda. Although this small representative selection (nos. 2.13–2.23) is fairly predictable, nevertheless, it does on occasion show a degree of imagination and inventiveness, which could be appreciated, even by those who would not share unionist's political aspirations.

In its most basic, simple form, the unionist message could be reduced to 'Ulster Will Fight' as shown in two of the better known postcards by the same unidentified artist sporting the initials, JVB (nos. 2.13 and 2.14). In the first of these, the artist or publisher has recruited a verse to the cause from a poem by one of the most celebrated living British poets of the early twentieth century, Algernon Charles Swinburne (1837–1909).

In the latter case, the doughty lass has of necessity taken a truly revolutionary step for the time by abandoning domesticity, symbolised by her discarded skein, to take up arms and follow the drum in defence of her cause – Ulster. In an age of supposed sexual equality, the pushing of women to the fore is hardly remarkable. A century ago it was rather more noteworthy, even if it was the era of the suffragettes.

2.13

2.14

This same general theme of fighting for the cause is restated with a shade more subtlety in several cartoons by another artist, William Watson (e.g. nos. 2.15 and 2.16). In the first example of this cartoonist's work, Ulster's defender, looking like a cross between a scoutmaster and a Mexican *bandido*, is literally armed to the teeth. There can be no doubt that he is fully prepared to defend 'Ulster' against Home Rule. It can hardly be a coincidence that his prisoner bears quite a good resemblance to contemporary photographs of John Redmond. Like his policy, he will be going nowhere!

In 'Home Rule Rout' (no. 2.16), Ulster's gallant guard-dog is shown protecting his flock, and sending the Home Rule fox into panic-stricken flight. This particular card is 'postally unused'. Therefore it is not possible to be certain if it represents a unionist celebration over the defeat of Home Rule. It could, on the other hand simply represent unionist wishful thinking, or even a threat as to how they will face the challenge, which that measure offered to their position and safety. The image of the defending bulldog is one which features in a number of other cards.

The prominent Union flag in both these and numerous other examples, no doubt represents the unionist belief that their campaign was the only way to retain the British link.

2.15

W. Watson.

Ulster Publishing Co.

Their apparent triumphalism is also a feature of no. 2.17 ('The Football Match') but it also reveals, along with further examples (nos. 2.18 and 2.19), a great deal more unionist insecurity and deep-seated fears. At the same time, it does lay out the outline for a cogently argued case against Home Rule.

It is hardly surprising that John Redmond comes off second best in his encounter with Edward Carson, as shown in this production (no. 2.17). Their conflict shows Carson staunchly defending Ulster's goal and forcefully repelling the attack of 'Tax Collector John' Edward Carson had long argued that it would be impossible to finance Home Rule without the taxable resources of Belfast. It was one of his strongest levers in trying to oppose the measure for the whole of Ireland.

Ulster, as shown, has a great deal defending, such as, 'Industry' and 'Prosperity'. Redmond for the rest of Ireland can offer only 'Sloth', 'Poverty', 'Boycott', 'Superstition', and 'Syndicalism'. Ulster he will try to buy with a dud cheque. Home Rule could hardly be less appealing!

The association of Home Rule with 'Syndicalism', or militant trade unionism was likely to have maximum effect on employers at this particular time, as there had been a series of strikes with violent repercussions in Britain and on the Continent in the years just before the First World War. Employers did not require long memories to recall the Belfast strike of 1907 nor the Dublin Lockout of 1913. In addition, a new triple alliance of railwaymen, miners and transport unions was formed in Britain in 1914, and it might quite conceivably paralyse the country in a future dispute.

The linking of Home Rule to this sort of activity was designed to strike terror into the hearts of all employers, and many of the prosperous middle class. No doubt, the threat of raised taxes was a threat to most, and the prospect of 'Poverty' would further strengthen unionist resolve.

Likewise, the reference to 'Boycott' would alarm landowners, against whom the tactic had sometimes been used from the 1880s, and the linking of Redmond to 'Superstition' played on Protestant fears of Catholicism. In short, this clever piece of propaganda managed to encapsulate many of the unionist objections to Home

Ulster Publishing Co.

2.16

2.17

Rule. 'Donegall Place Under Home Rule' (no. 2.18) puts forward some of the same arguments with more vivid examples.

This is probably the best known of all the propaganda postcards issued by the Unionists during the 1912–14 campaign against the Third Home Rule Bill. In it, the anonymous cartoonist envisages the sorry plight of Belfast, and by implication 'Ulster', under the Home Rule parliament.

The newly erected City Hall (since 1906), pride and joy of Belfast unionists, is no longer in pristine condition. Now, under an Irish flag, it lies derelict and the workhouse overshadows everything. What was formerly the well-known Robinson and Cleaver's department store is 'To Let', while farmyard animals graze in the very heart of Belfast, with Donegall Place now on offer 'For Pasture'.

DONEGALL PLACE, BELFAST, UNDER HOME RULE. 2.18

The new Ireland under Home Rule is no longer represented by the statues of British royalty, but by nationalist figures, such as 'Skin the Goat' (Fitzharris), a noted Fenian allegedly involved in the Phoenix Park murders, in the company of Home Rule leaders, Redmond and Dillon. Incidentally, an alternative version has Joe Devlin, the West Belfast Home Rule MP instead of Dillon. It is worth imagining for a moment a hypothetical proposal to replace Queen Victoria's statue near the City Hall with one of the modern-day holder, until quite recently, of Devlin's seat, namely Gerry Adams. Would it not lead to an interesting and heated City Council discussion?

The figure of 'Boer War McBride', nearest to Robinson and Cleaver's, is of particular potency. Major McBride, husband of the more widely known Maud Gonne, later to be executed for his part in the 1916 Rising, had particularly incurred the wrath of unionists by his involvement in the Boer War (1899–1902). Obviously it had galled the British also, as it later formed part of his indictment after the 1916 Rising. During the African war, he had helped organise an Irish Brigade to fight against the British. The fact that it had made no military impact did nothing to lessen the hostility with which he was viewed by unionists.

Faced with the grim prophecies depicted in this card, unionists would feel justified in uttering their war-cry 'Ulster will fight. Ulster will be right'. Unionist fears, as expressed here, again surface in the scene at Carrickfergus Castle (no. 2.19), at the Albert Clock, and in similar pictures of other Ulster towns, imagining their fate under Home Rule.

Similar cards, some of them very rare indeed, have been identified for the following provincial towns; Bangor, Ballymena, Carrickfergus, Downpatrick, Dungannon, Londonderry (see cover), Lurgan, Newry, Omagh and Portadown, while examples for other towns may also exist.

The strength of that localised approach was that the threat to local 'monuments' would pose a very real and immediate threat in the eyes of local unionists, as opposed to something remote and generalised, and was consequently all the more likely to involve them actively in opposition to Home Rule.

According to the artist in no. 2.19, the prosperity of the town is ruined, just like the sunken boat. The statue of John Redmond, the new King of Ireland (REX HIBERNIAE) has replaced King Billy in this his formerly loyal stronghold. The graffiti artist expresses his own political views with his irreverent version of the Latin inscription on the plinth, 'REDMOND WRECKS HIBERNIA'.

Sober Carrickfergus is now defiled with the Harbour Bar, whose proprietor (PROPER RIOTER) is revealed to be none other than the nationalist MP, National President of the Irish section of the Hibernians since 1905, and unionist hate-figure, Joe Devlin. The public house advertises 'FINE OLD PORT', its play on words no doubt a reference to the town's former prosperity, before the advent of this dreadful Home Rule. All unionists would have been aware of the town's association with William of Orange, and many would also have known of its prominence as a port especially throughout the eighteenth century.

Now that the centre-piece of the town, its castle, is in the hands of the Ancient Order of Hibernians, the Irish militia and the Molly Maguires, one of the agrarian secret societies whose members attacked mainly Protestant landlords and their property, it supports Irish rather than British industry, and flies a collection of Irish nationalist flags. The harbour, on which the town's prosperity had depended, has now become a dumping ground for rubbish, including 'LANDLORDS AND ULSTER-SCOTS'. Such was the alarming threat of Home Rule, as spelled out in this clever piece of sustained imagery.

2.19

The Albert Clock, which is the centre-piece of no. 2.20 is amongst Belfast's best known landmarks. On its completion in 1869, it was dedicated to Prince Albert, the Consort of Queen Victoria. Because of its association with the monarchy, this monument would have a particularly warm spot in the hearts of Ulster loyalists.

To witness its destruction, especially to make way for a statue of the hated John Redmond, would be an appalling prospect for any unionist. The propagandist here forecasts that as one outcome of Home Rule.

The Custom House, whose steps were traditionally used as a podium by Protestant street preachers, has now become the offices of the Molly Maguires (cf. no. 2.19). As a result of the new political regime, poverty is rife, to such an extent that even the Poor House Annex is full. Protestants are left with little option but to queue at the Protestant Emigration Office, which offers them 'TICKETS FOR NEW YORK OR ANYWHERE'.

Time is short as the ship waits under the Stars and Stripes. A sandwich man, until the 1960s at least, a common feature on Belfast's streets, advertises a 'CLEARANCE SALE', while farmyard animals graze in the formerly busy thoroughfare, which shares a fate similar to Donegall Place under Home Rule (no. 16). Symbols of royalty as well as their religion and economic well-being have all been depicted as under grave threat. If this was to be the future under Home Rule, then all the unionist demonstrations and threats of violence described elsewhere in this chapter, (e.g. nos. 2.2, 2.4 and 2.5) could easily be justified.

In contrast to the last three examples, which depend heavily for their impact on knowledge of Irish history, card no. 2.21 is directed more towards an English, rather than an Ulster, audience, although some of it would likely go over their heads unless

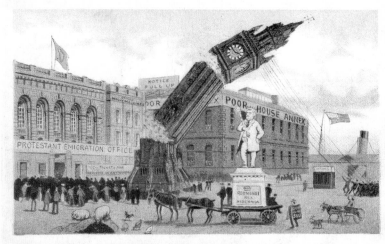

BELFAST UNDER HOME RULE.   Making a Site for the Statue of King John the First of Ireland.   2.20

2.21

they had some knowledge of Irish history. It represents an appeal to John Bull to save Ulster, in particular, by holding on firmly lest Ireland should be cast adrift and find herself dashed against the Home Rule rocks. From the viewpoint of the artist, only the parliament at Westminster could make the crucial decision by rejecting Home Rule. The cry 'Don't Let Go' conveys a sense of panic that that was exactly what was about to happen.

Amongst the various political references on the card, the most significant are probably the names given to the Irish provinces. Ulster (nine counties incidentally) is dubbed, 'Prosperity Province'. It is to protect and retain this relative prosperity that 'No Surrender Forts' are manned by Ulster loyalists.

Nobody could disagree with the naming of Connacht as 'Poverty Province', as it has traditionally been, and certainly remains, with the exception of pockets like Galway city, the poorest part of Ireland. Of course, the motive in this case, for so naming it was to highlight the comparison with Ulster prosperity, and to allege that the threatened 'letting go', i.e. Home Rule, would reduce the Ulster economy to the level of the western province.

'The Land League Province' of Munster was meant to publicise the threat to the rights and prosperity of landlords. The reference to Leinster as 'Maynooth Province', after the famous seminary for the training of Catholic priests, was a marginally more subtle way of expressing the well-worn unionist slogan, 'Home Rule is Rome Rule'.

In a nutshell, this appeal to British opinion does not differ significantly from the appeal to their own unionist supporters in Ulster. Their case against Home Rule remained much the same, namely that it would weaken or even destroy the Union, and lead to an impoverished, priest-ridden Ireland.

Religion was clearly a significant theme in many cards and has been referred to in passing in a generalised fashion. In fact some leading unionist figures, such as J. Milne Barbour, would pinpoint it as *the key* issue for unionists (see Lee p. 8). Contemporary postcards can neither prove nor disprove this, but extracts from a number of cards reveal in better detail what exactly were their fears.

In the first instance, the Protestant reaction was mainly defensive. Undoubtedly they saw themselves as historically under siege from Rome, as described in extracts from other cards not reproduced here:

> Here let us say, when our freedom is threatened,
> That Rome we'll not trust no more we would Satan
> For history has told us, and by the same token,
> In spite of all promise she'd make slaves of us all.
>   (from 'Sir Edward, My Boy!', Exchange Publishing Co.)

And yet again:

> This land our heritage by richt
> Priest ridden Saints may grudge us
>   (from 'The Ulster-Scot', Ulster Publishing Co.)

No assurances from the likes of Redmond would assuage these fears. It is worth stressing that they were shared (as shown in another card) by the educated Protestant Church leadership of the time. Notwithstanding the sincerity of Catholic individuals, Rome as an institution could not be trusted in their eyes (see Lee, p. 16). Historical evidence of threat was quoted is the form of the Jesuits, a leading force of the Counter-Reformation, and the Armada, a physical threat, and the continuity of that threat was highlighted by reference to the recent *Ne Temere* decree (from a card entitled 'Sir Edward Carson's Bulldog Ulster', Ulster Publishing Co.), which threatened the Protestant religious birthright of children in a mixed marriage. In some cases the propaganda in these cards goes well beyond the defensive to the offensive in all senses of the word.

What is the key to summing up all these cards? Obviously as well as providing a vivid pictorial and contemporary record of much of the opposition to Home Rule, they reveal evidence of Ulster Unionist motivation, whether political, religious or economic. Do they prioritise these motives? To that question there is no definitive answer. The mixture of motives could be as great as the number of interested individuals. At best only a somewhat tentative conclusion can be drawn.

The prominent Union flag in many of the examples is often a symbol of defiance, but it is also a symbol of loyalty and belonging. It is argued here that the flag-wavers and many of the postcard producers disguise an underlying fear. For Unionists such as Balfour and many others, there could be not be 'any real half-

2.22

Neighbour—"Where are ye drivin' him to, Johnny?"
Redmond—"Whisht, ye Divil ye! It's Home Rule he thinks we're goin' to; but it's Separation I'm drivin' him to."

way house between the Union and a complete separation in Anglo-Irish relations', (Dutton, p. 210). Other historians, such as J.J. Lee recognise this fear, but make it of secondary importance to 'violated machismo' or what one might call a threat to the Unionist superiority complex. This writer would lean more towards the earlier Balfour interpretation, and if that is correct it lends great significance to this postcard (no. 2.22).

If Redmond were a false prophet leading Ireland to the real destination of 'Separation' and not 'Home Rule', then the entire dreaded political, religious and economic disadvantage illustrated in some of the other cards would follow. This is the very crux of the matter. This fear was implied in the earlier example, 'Don't Let Go' and was even more clearly and emotionally enunciated in the plaintive, 'Intreat me not to leave thee', drawn from the Old Testament, book of Ruth, and quoting verses 1–16 on the reverse (no. 2.23). It was issued at least twice as a political postcard, once in a sepia version and again in colour.

2.23

2.24

HOME RULE DEMONSTRATION, DUBLIN, 31st MARCH, 1912.
National University Platform—Professor J. G. Swift McNeill, M.P. addressing the meeting.
Published by Eason & Son, Ltd., Dublin and Belfast.   Photo. Keogh Bros.

> Intreat me not to leave thee,or to return from following after thee:
> For whither thou goest, I will go;
> And where thou lodgest, I will lodge;
> thy people shall be my people, and thy God my God.

This heartfelt appeal, which was directed at the British government, was accompanied by an adaptation of Calderon's painting "Naomi and Ruth" from the Warwick Gallery in Liverpool.

* * * * *

Enough of the unionist case, which has been analysed in considerable detail, but what of their opponents? There are far fewer cards in favour of Home Rule. The fact that Redmond, as historians such as Lee have pointed out, did not take Unionist opposition seriously must be a contributory factor. Redmond believed that the withdrawal of British political support would for the most part end Unionist opposition. In any case, what really mattered, as far as he was concerned, was the government at Westminster, and there the case appeared to be won by 1912. Insofar as the issue had to be argued, Westminster was the place to do it.

Consequently extra-parliamentary propaganda was of minor significance. Despite this there were some pro-Home Rule postcards. Compared to those of their opponents, in general they are much less strident in tone. Given the political scenario in parliament, a certain smugness on the part of supporters of the measure is understandable.

2.25

Some of these productions are no more than photographic records of Home Rule rallies (for example, no. 2.24), a mirror image of their opponents' marches. They do not say much except to point out that Home Rulers, like their opponents, could muster crowds of supporters. Others cards, such as no. 2.25, paint a romantic, happy picture of Ireland under Home Rule. The ruined monastery sits in peaceful splendour, bordering a placid sea, and bathed in a Celtic sunset. A young lad, carrying his Home Rule placard or banner, stands with his beloved dog in these peaceful, idyllic surroundings.

One could be forgiven for taking this young man to be a contented Irish leprechaun, for surely his style of dress would have been a source of considerable amusement anywhere in Ireland apart from a stage set! Although the presentation seems terribly dated a century later, its theatricality should be seen in the context of a cultural revival flavoured by Yeats' 'Celtic Twilight'.

Perhaps this picture is meant for Irish-American consumption, emphasising how happy Ireland will be at last, now that she is at least partly in charge of her own affairs. The young boy bears a closer relation to Fifth Avenue, New York, on Saint Patrick's Day than to any mortal likely to be found in Ireland.

Interestingly, this card illustrates how a large commercial concern, and a producer of many political cards, like Valentine's, could adapt its stock to save costs and widen its commercial appeal. Common motifs, mottos and graphics were interchanged. What probably started life as a non-political, sentimental product designed for Irish emigrants and their relatives (no. 2.26) has been adjusted to fit in with the current political movement for Home Rule (nos. 2.27 and 2.28 and even the concertina within no. 2.1).

"Erin Sings her Old Songs."

"Come Back to Erin."

2.26

All the cards featured in this section date from the period 1912–14. One of the major artistic fashions stretching from the latter years of the nineteenth century had been the Art Nouveau movement. Although it is of no great consequence, it might be observed here in passing that the sunburst used in all these cards was a regular feature of that particular style.

2.26

Cats were another common feature in postcards. They were so popular on postcards in general that they are often seen as a separate category for collectors. The most famous artist associated with cat pictures was Louis Wain, for whom they became an unfortunate and unhealthy obsession.

It should come as no great surprise then that they were pressed into political service in postcard form. The card numbered 2.29 is a sample from a series of Home Rule postcards designed to appeal to cat-lovers. Many would no doubt find them cute and cuddly. To others, they may well appear bland, insipid and ineffective as political propaganda. While not wishing to appear sexist, the thought occurs that the use of cats may be an attempt to

2.27

44

appeal especially to the feminine market. Certainly cats were also employed in suffragette postcards at this time.

Home Rule was newsworthy as one of the major political issues of the time. For some cartoonists, irrespective of their political views, it became a handy vehicle for humour. This applies to more than one piece of work from Donald McGill, one of the most famous of all postcard artists, who produced an estimated 10,000 designs in a career spanning fifty years. He is known to have produced at least six cards on this topic.

Since 1800, the Act of Union, placing Ireland under the direct political authority of Westminster, had met with both constitutional and violent opposition in Ireland. Widespread support for Daniel O'Connell in the 1840s, and later for the Home Rule campaigns of the Irish Parliamentary Party in 1886 provided evidence that the Act was an unpopular measure.

In this example (no. 2.30), McGill comments on the third Home Rule bill of 1912. Wittily he compares Home Rule to a kiss, 'An Act Of Union Which Satisfies Both Parties.' The young man in his green coat and the young lady in her red, white and blue both seem highly contented with their lot!

Whatever the cartoonist's intention, the claim that Home Rule would strengthen the existing close links between Britain and Ireland, accords with the view of John

2.28

"WE SHALL BEGIN TO LOOK UP NOW!"

2.29

2.30

Redmond, and challenges the commonly-expressed unionist notion that Home Rule would damage, or even destroy the Union. That argument has been well illustrated in several postcards described here previously. It is an argument which can even be traced back to the time of O'Connell's Repeal Campaign, although not in the form of postcards, of course. Opponents of O'Connell had also argued that his real plan was separation, while he had insisted that the re-establishment of an Irish legislature would more firmly cement Irish loyalty to the British link. It would certainly be difficult to challenge the view that Home Rule would have had majority support in Ireland at this time. Whether it would have strengthened or weakened the Union cannot be proven.

However, it is highly likely that McGill was much more interested in the humour than in scoring political points. The same is probably true of some further examples (nos. 2.31 and 2.32). In the first of these, the humorous allusion to Home Rule is in all probability, an oblique reference to a concurrent political issue, namely the campaign for women's suffrage.

2.31

PADDY under HOME-RULE.

2.32

In England, the Women's Social and Political Union, founded in 1903, relied initially upon propaganda and disruption to make its case. By 1912, they had embarked on a programme of small-scale violence.

In Ireland, the Irish Women's Franchise League had been established since 1908, and the Irish Women's Suffrage Federation since 1911. Hannah Sheehy-Skeffington, one of the founder members of the former organisation, and others were imprisoned for smashing windows in protest that the Home Rule Bill ignored the demand for women's suffrage. Both the content and the dating of this particular card, postmarked May 1912, cement the conclusion that the cartoonist is making a link between the two issues.

Once again in no. 2.32, the poor Irishman has discovered to his cost the real meaning of 'Home Rule'. Years of effort have produced a rather unexpected outcome! This card, issued by Lawrences of Dublin, in its gentle humour, hints at male resignation in the face of overwhelming odds. While 'his lordship' washes the clothes, the female 'master of the house' peruses the newspaper! The humour in our final selection (no. 2.33) might not have been taken in such good spirit, since it smacks just a bit too much of traditional English arrogance, as displayed towards the Irish in some of the cartoons of *Punch*. The poor Irish caveman is not far removed from the earlier ape-like depiction of Irish nationalists in that journal.

To conclude, postcards were used to illustrate marches, meetings and rallies of Home Rulers and their opponents. They were also used very effectively by unionists, and considerably less so by nationalists, to argue the pros and cons of the case. Unionist opposition to Home Rule was not only described, but also explained in some detail. To convey their message, they certainly followed their commitment from the Ulster Covenant to use 'all means', for we have seen how they drew inspiration from and made effective use of the Bible, of pre-existing poetry, art and songs, of newly composed verse, of artists' impressions, and not least of cartoons. Their propaganda focused on the British mainland opinion, on loyal Ulster in general, and on a localised appeal.

2.33

Of course, it can be argued that none of this would have mattered without accompanying actions, without mass drilling and gun-running, for example, but the question can also be asked would this have happened to such an extent and with such support without the widespread inspiration and propaganda of postcards.

By 1914, whether in jest or deadly earnest, Home Rule, as a major issue in British politics, had provided rich subject matter for photographers, artists and cartoonists. Then its importance receded rapidly, when a much greater crisis, the Great War, tore Europe apart and radically altered much more than the history of Ireland. However, the new situation was to provide continuing opportunities for the postcard propagandist.

3

IRELAND AND THE FIRST WORLD WAR

Introduction

It would not be feasible to study postcards relating to the Great War, the Easter Rising and the revival of Sinn Féin within a single chapter. The Rising would scarcely have happened without the War, and both were major factors in the later rise of Sinn Féin. Close linkage between the three can be observed in postcards produced, and it is sometimes problematical as to how some cards should be categorised. Nevertheless, a number of cards on the Rising and those relating to the other themes are sufficiently distinctive to justify the decision to treat the closely linked topics separately.

One important distinction needs to be drawn between postcards on the Home Rule crisis and those relevant to the First World War, the 1916 Rising and the rise of Sinn Féin. In the former case postcards form the greatest proportion of printed propagandist material. In all the other cases, they form but one strand of a stream of material, which includes a 'flood of rebel memorabilia', 'of postcards, mass cards, song sheets, pamphlets, flags, badges, pictures, photograph albums, calendars, and a host of other mass-produced items.' (Hart, p. 207) While there is no desire to study the other material at any length here, reference should be made to it, in order to set the cards in context, and because each often complements the other.

The outbreak of the Great War in 1914 had an immediate impact on both Redmond and Carson's followers. Although both the Ulster Volunteers and the Irish Volunteers had very recently imported arms from Germany, each of the political leaders had been eager to proclaim his loyalty to Britain. A cynic might say that a short victorious war was expected and that it was good politics to do so.

Home Rule, despite its importance as an issue, was now a distraction. Compromise between Redmond and Carson had proved impossible as recently as the Buckingham Palace Conference, convened in late July 1914. Now it was expedient for both. The Home Rule Bill, so recently a cause of bitter contention, was neatly shunted aside in September, when it was passed into law, but was also suspended for the duration of the War.

The mothballed aspirations of each leader remained unchanged. Redmond expected Home Rule as a reward for his loyalty. Carson, on the other hand, hoped that it would be abandoned, or failing that, as a poor second best, that Ulster would at least be excluded.

3.1   3.2

At least 200,000 Irishmen fought in the British Army during the First World War, although that fact has frequently been overlooked, at least until recently, often with a political motivation. The deeds and sacrifice of the 36th Ulster Division have been highlighted regularly, but sometimes at the expense of other Irish involvement in the war.

Irishmen, many of them nationalists, fought and died at several locations on the Western Front as well as in Gallipoli, Salonika, and Palestine. In total, about 30,000 gave their lives during the various campaigns (see discussion in Jeffery p. 150. among others, for example Philip Orr, who used similar figures of 30,000 to 35,000 in *Our War: Ireland and The Great War* (p. 76), J. Horne (ed.), Dublin 2008). But there was also significant, and as time went on, growing opposition to Irish participation. Contemporary postcards reflect some of the disagreement and at least make it possible to form a reasonably rounded view of Irish attitudes towards the war.

* * * * *

New political developments, resulting from the outbreak of the Great War, are reflected in 'The Day' (no. 3.1) and in 'Shure he thought we were Traitors' (no. 3.2).

In the former, reflecting the position pre-August 1914, Redmond and Carson, with sleeves rolled up for action, square up to each other, while the Kaiser smilingly oversees the proceedings. Ireland, beset with civil war, between nationalists and loyalists, would create a serious distraction for Britain, and a most favourable scenario for Germany about to go to war with her great naval and commercial rival.

The sequel, (no. 3.2) tells a very different story. Now that war has broken out, each of the respective Irish leaders were followed by a column of uniformed marching men. That which comes from Belfast represents the 36th Ulster Division – the old UVF – which volunteered *en masse* for service in 1914. Those who follow Redmond represent the majority of the Irish Volunteers who supported Redmond's call to arms in his Woodenbridge speech of September 1914.

The Kaiser was entitled to hope that an Irish conflict would prove a serious hindrance to Britain's war effort, as nationalists and unionists confronted each other with their newly acquired German arms (no. 3.1). Instead their leaders clasp hands in friendship and support a common cause in fighting for Britain. Faced with this new situation, he exits discomfited (no. 3.2).

In a similar fashion, this further example (no. 3.3), also approvingly compares the actions of two bodies of Irish Volunteers, but this time from two different eras.

3.3

3.4

Here the parallel is drawn between the Volunteers of 1780 and their counterparts in 1914. Both forces had been formed to campaign for the redress of Irish grievances. The former group was established in 1779 to demand the end of trade restrictions imposed on Ireland by the Westminster parliament. In addition they argued that the Irish parliament should be allowed increased legislative powers.

The more recent group sought to pressurise the British into re-establishing that parliament, which had been abolished by the Act of Union of 1800. Each force would have seen itself as a protector of Ireland. On both occasions, there was a theoretical, if somewhat remote possibility, that Ireland needed defending from a threat of foreign invasion.

By 1780, in fact France had already committed itself to the cause of the American colonists in their revolt against the British Crown. An attack on Britain through the Irish backdoor was possible in 1780, just as a German invasion in 1914 could not be totally discounted. A proposal to land an invasion force in the west of Ireland was actually considered but rejected by the German High Command.

In reality, however, Irish support for Germany was negligible beyond the republican fringe. A picture of the two main leaders of political opinion in Ireland linking each other in apparent friendship beneath the crossed Union Jack and Irish harp flags reinforces this point (no. 3.4).

The real impact of the card lies within the caption in the single word 'NOW'. It marks the contrast with the period 1912–14, when Redmond and Carson had been the bitterest of political enemies, as chief proponent and opponent of Home Rule (see no. 1 for example). A very similar card showing both leaders uniformed and raising the standard, includes the verse 'Patriots All.'

Begorra, but ye thocht Oi was going to be a thraitor.

3.5

Begorra, and he thocht to catch me bending.

3.6

Patriots All

United in defence they stand,
North and South for Motherland,
When peace comes with healing wand,
May they, as now, be hand in hand!

It would appear that both authors are also attempting to forecast a future after the war, when their strategies would once again diverge. In a way, they would have been correct, but little could they have known, that political events such as the 1916 Rising and its aftermath would render both their original policies on Home Rule obsolete, at least for a majority of Irishmen.

Frustrated German ambitions in Ireland were once again highlighted by the major British postcard publisher, Bamforth and Co. in some of its War Cartoon series. While the theme here (nos. 3.5 and 3.6) was very similar to no. 3.2, the presentation in both these samples lacked any of the subtlety of the former example, and smacked much more of stage Irishness. In any case, these and indeed other cards clearly illustrated the pro-British sentiment of many Irishmen at that time. There is no doubt that this went well beyond a grudging support for the war.

Obviously all these cards express pro-war sentiments, but whether they should be called propagandist is a moot point. They are really reactive. Their main purpose would seem to be showing approval for Redmond's support of the war effort, rather than to be proactive recruiting propaganda. Such propaganda certainly existed and in large measure, but it was conducted mainly through posters, leaflets and recruiting meetings rather than postcards.

With or without propaganda, there was apparently considerable enthusiasm within Ireland for the war effort, and one does not really need to rely upon the evidence of this card alone (no. 3.7). Here the jingoistic message is plain, simple and

3.7

**WITH COMPLIMENTS FROM
THE IRISH BRIGADE TO THE PRUSSIAN GUARD**

and with many compliments to the
Jrish Brigade from
Louis Raemaekers

direct, namely that the Irish troops in the British Army will put the Germans, especially the traditionally elite and militaristic Prussians, in their place.

The artist in this case was Louis Raemaekers (1868–1956), a Dutch political cartoonist. During the First World War, he became well-known for his propagandist cartoons. The general theme of several of these was the accusation that Germans were guilty of atrocities. Given the generally propagandist-nature of the artist's work, this particular example, which was produced to benefit the Employment Bureau for Disabled Irish Soldiers and Sailors in Dublin, should be interpreted with a degree of caution, even greater than one would normally reserve for all wartime publicity.

Strictly speaking, although the term was in common usage, there was no such Irish army grouping as 'The Irish Brigade' between 1914 and 1918. Raemaekers has used the name as a convenient collective term for all the Irish regiments fighting in the First World War. These would have been made up of soldiers from all over Ireland, including those in, for example, the Ulster Rifles, the Inniskillings, the Irish Guards, the Munster Rifles, the Connaught Rangers and the Dublin Fusiliers. This particular sample is very similar in style, theme and purpose to the work of the Belfast artist, William Conor, who designed two cards, the proceeds of which were used to fund the UVF Hospital at Shaftesbury Square, Belfast.

A Hopeful
Christmas
and
Victorious
New Year!

At Thiepval, 1st July, 1916.

Charge of the Ulster Division.

"When I saw the Ulstermen emerge through the smoke and form
up as on parade, I could hardly believe my eyes. Then I saw them
attack, beginning at a slow walk over no-man's land, and then
suddenly let loose as they charged over the two front lines of the
enemy's trenches, shouting 'No Surrender!'"—*The Times.*

3.8

One of the pair (no. 3.8), apparently designed as a Christmas card, conveyed the artist's impression of the Ulster Division's advance on the Somme in July 1916. This imaginative reconstruction is accompanied by an extract from the *Times*. In that assault, their casualties were horrendous, as was highlighted in a contemporary letter from Major Singleton of the Ulster Division's Field Headquarters: '… our effort was not for absolutely nothing BUT our casualties for so little appear terrible. … And now, the Ulster Division has practically ceased to exist.'

At least Conor showed a touch of realism in wishing us a 'Hopeful' rather than a 'Happy' Christmas. Even this modest hint of realism was not present in the depiction of a supposedly typical Ulster Volunteer (no. 3.9), who risked

3.9

such a dreadful and almost inevitable fate. Hardly surprisingly, since this was again propaganda like most of the other examples chosen, the volunteer's pristine uniform conveys nothing of the horrors of the front.

There are many gruesome photographs of life and death at the front, as anyone who has visited war museums in Belgium will know, but no postcards of realistic 'action shots' could be traced. The nearest that we come to these would be the somewhat anaemic *Daily Mail* official war pictures. All of these carry the notice 'Passed by Censor'. They include a few of Irish interest. For example, 'The Irish Brigade returning from Guillemont' comes to mind. These are probably best considered as soft-core propaganda.

The real war, that is the war of attrition, which postcards failed to describe, because neither censorship nor commercial sense would allow it, was such that even the enthusiasm of some volunteers, and the propaganda depicted in most of these cards, failed to produce troops in the numbers required. One obvious solution would have been to extend conscription to Ireland. Widespread resistance to that proposal later gave Sinn Féin scope to attack the Redmondite policy of supporting the war effort (see further on this subject in chapter 5).

In no. 3.10, Britain offers Home Rule but the gift has a high and hidden price, namely the scourge of conscription, which was unacceptable to a wide range of Irish people. Before the offer of a 'Home Rule,' Christmas card from Britain, the maiden

(Ireland) stands aloof. She bears in her right hand the sword of Sinn Féin policy, while her left clutches to her breast a scroll inscribed 'Ireland for the Irish.' By clear implication, others such as Redmond, might have been fooled or bought off by British blandishments, but certainly not Sinn Féin.

Both enthusiasm for the war effort, at least in its early stages, as well as resistance to enlistment were a reality. It is safe to say that supporters and opponents alike each exaggerated their case. The efforts, supposedly required to mobilise Irish conscripts were depicted in a postcard series (e.g. no. 3.11), and in a similar fashion (no. 3.12) claims to show the ridiculous lengths to which the British establishment must go with their Drilling Sergeant's Tower to enforce an Irish conscript's compliance with military drill.

Copyright.]   [Published by J. J. P. O'Healy, 23 Bachelor's Walk.

The Compliment of the Season!

3.10

Although the images in both cases are far-fetched, their underlying point is clearly not without validity. Lloyd George himself, Prime Minister from December 1916, recognised the difficulty in applying the policy of conscription to Ireland when he warned that Irish conscripts would be recruited 'at the point of a bayonet.'

During most wars, governments have assumed emergency powers. The Great War was no exception when Defence of the Realm Acts, or DORA, were passed from 1914 onwards. Because they curtailed people's rights, these acts were criticised. Not surprisingly, criticism in Ireland was especially fierce (no.3.13). It was under this legislation that republicans had been arrested and tried after the 1916 Rising. Later, when republicans had reorganised both the Volunteers and Sinn Féin, the acts were once again used against them.

This particular card pours scorn on 'Gentle D.O.R.A.' (possibly a play on the roughly contemporary ballad, 'Gentle Nora'), under which some harmless yokels and their dog have been apprehended. As the full range of the military arsenal including airships, biplanes, armoured cars and even tanks is launched against the defenceless peasants, farmyard animals and fowl scatter. As soldiers advance towards the yard, police observe and take notes from the safety of the perimeter wall. The wall itself is plastered with a plethora of posters, 'A Proclamation', 'A Special Proclamation', and 'A Proclamation Against Illegal Drilling.'

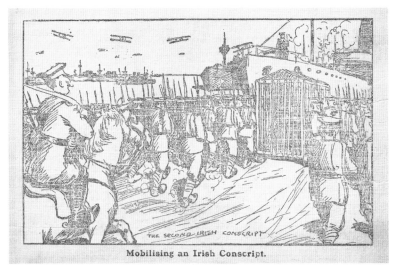

Mobilising an Irish Conscript.

3.11

DRILLING AN IRISH CONSCRIPT.

3.12

This card dates from late in the war, most likely during the second half of 1918. Although tanks had been developed some time earlier, they were first used effectively at the Battle of Cambrai late in 1917. Lord French, in whose name 'Another Proclamation' was issued, did not become Lord Lieutenant of Ireland until May 1918. This card is also a further illustration of how different media complemented each other. Peadar Ó Cearnaigh, the republican balladeer, represented DORA as a sort of British *femme fatale* on a cover sheet for one of his contemporary tunes. Her 'gentleness', referred to in this card's title, is loaded with irony.

Since a thorough examination of these cards (nos. 3.11, 3.12 and 3.13), reveals neither a publisher's name nor a cartoonist's identity, it is just conceivable that they

GENTLE D. O. R. A.

3.13

are not politically motivated, but rather seek to highlight the contemporary Irish political scene in a comical fashion. However, it is much more likely that they are following the advanced nationalist agenda by pouring scorn on British policy in Ireland.

Even for those who might not have any particular love for the separatist ideas of Sinn Féin, there is extensive evidence to suggest that a growing disillusionment with British policy had set in before the end of the War. Any propaganda in tune with this public mindset and emotion was almost certain to have an impact. All the more radical Irish nationalists who opposed Irish participation in the War were likely to gain support from this changing public opinion. In 'Put these on like a good little boy ...', we are shown a sequence of events (no. 3.14). The little boy on the left, in the sailor suit, has his hands raised reaching out for 'freedom.' He represents Ireland in or about 1914. In the centre section he is encouraged by Britannia to join the armed forces. Along with the uniform he is offered land. The acceptance of the invitation to don the uniform is clearly fraught with great danger. Britannia, who makes the offer and the promise of a 'cake', is shown with the head of a skeleton. Finally, the boy on the right, again representing Ireland, now protests vociferously about Britain's failure to keep her promise. He has responded to Britain's call to arms, as did many nationalists, but he has not been rewarded as promised.

Ireland had been promised Home Rule in 1912. By 1914, following the threat of revolt (including the possible use of force of arms) by unionists, and the outbreak of the First World War, the Bill had been put on hold, subject to the ending of the war, and a satisfactory resolution of the Ulster Question. This card could be seen as reflecting the impatience and disappointment of the Redmondites – that their

Britannia—"Put these on, like a good little boy, and I'll promise you a nice cake of land."

3.14

expectations of Home Rule as a reward for their participation in the war, was not now being met. However, on the strength of other work by this same artist (who signs himself 'Seaghan', 'Sean Mac Murchadha' or simply 'Sean M.'), it is much more likely that the Irish Parliamentary Party, although never mentioned by name, was by implication just as much the subject of attack as the deadly deceptive Britannia.

The same holds true for 'The Promised Land,' another work of the same cartoonist, and most likely sold as one of the same set of postcards (no. 3.15). One card is needed to complement the other. Otherwise the meaning of the latter card in isolation would be quite obscure. It can be seen as Britain's reply to the child's

THE PROMISED LAND.

3.15

cry, and the outcome of listening to Redmond and his followers' encouragement to enlist. If one can lambast opponents without even referring to them by name, then surely that touches the very pinnacle of the political cartoonist's art. In its bleak and stark simplicity, 'ONE MAN'S LAND' requires no further explanation, but remains a grim and chilling image almost a century later. However, it might also be suggested that the title, with the scene of desolation depicted, is meant to suggest no man's land between the trenches of the First World War.

Further disappointment was the lot of all those nationalists who expected that the ending of war in 1918 would give them their desired settlement. In November, after the Armistice, a Peace Conference was arranged, and in 1919 representatives of the nations met in the famous Hall of Mirrors at Versailles. There was no sign of Home Rule for the Irish Parliamentary Party, but Sinn Féin retained high, if unrealistic, hopes.

Reinforced by the widespread claim that the recent war had been fought 'for the freedom of small nations', Sinn Féin reckoned that Ireland's case for independence could and should be put forward. As early as December 1918, the Sinn Féin Election Manifesto stated the means by which the Party intended to achieve an independent Irish republic, and these included, 'By appealing to the Peace Conference for the establishment of Ireland as an Independent Nation ... .'

Count Plunkett, father of Joseph Plunkett, one of the executed 1916 leaders, was amongst those dispatched to represent Ireland. In his 1919 letter to the French premier, George Clemenceau, Sean T. O'Kelly stated that the aim of the Irish delegation (O'Kelly plus Griffith, De Valera and Plunkett) was:

> to establish formally and definitely before the Peace Conference and the League of Nations Commission now assembled in Paris, Ireland's indisputable rights to international recognition for her independence and the propriety of her claim to enter the League of Nations as one of its constituent members.

This fanciful picture (no. 3.16) shows the empty chair reserved for Éire, about to make her grand entrance to join the international dignitaries. At least one other card very similar to this was produced at the time. In effect, matters of global politics ensured that Plunkett and his colleagues made no progress, and international recognition was not forthcoming. In particular, President Wilson of the USA, who had espoused the principle of self-determination in his Fourteen Points of January 1918, had no intention of jeopardising his relationship with Britain because of some vague sympathy with Ireland.

Looked at objectively, the Sinn Féin policy now looks like fantasy. Could they have any realistic expectation that Britain would accede to pressure from USA, even if it did exist, which is highly doubtful, or from anywhere else for that matter, to

3.16

UP PLUNKETT !

meet Irish secessionists' demands, given that they had consistently opposed the War, had colluded with Germany, had opposed Conscription, and above all had launched a rebellion in 1916?

In the meantime, events in Ireland between 1916 and 1918 had ensured that Home Rule, the preferred solution of most Irishmen prior to the Great War, was unlikely to prove an acceptable solution in its aftermath. That policy had now become outdated following the Easter Rising (see chapter 4) and the rise of a new Sinn Féin (see chapter 5).

In conclusion, pro-war postcards praised and encouraged Irish enlistment, and praised the prowess of Irish soldiers. Anti-war cards opposed enlistment and criticised British duplicity, as well as the efforts of Irish supporters of Irish recruitment. Nevertheless, in no card was criticism found of the recruits themselves.

Criticism of Britain was clear and specific. She offered Home Rule. Instead she delivered death, while Irish self-determination and the struggle 'for the freedom of small nations', were depicted as yet more false promises to induce Irishmen to join the British forces.

4

THE EASTER RISING

Introduction

Ulster Unionists and constitutional nationalists such as Redmond had seen the Great War as an opportunity to further their political aims. Likewise Irish separatists, sought to exploit the situation to achieve their own political ends through a violent rising.

The planning of this revolt was conducted from 1915 by the self-appointed inner circle, dubbed the Military Council of the IRB. Having brought James Connolly into their plans, their main strike force was intended to be the Irish Volunteers, that is, the minority of the original force from 1913 who had refused to follow Redmond in supporting the British war effort. This force was to be augmented by the much smaller Irish Citizen Army.

The Rising, originally planned for Easter Sunday, was launched in a truncated form on Easter Monday. The change of plan was made necessary by a series of organisational disasters for the rebels. Most notable of these were the arrest of Sir Roger Casement, the loss of their German arms supply on the scuttling of the *Aud*, and above all else, the cancelling of all Easter Sunday manoeuvres, which the plotters had planned to use as cover for the rebellion.

Although Pearse and the other organisers had planned to use the 15,000 strong Volunteers, they had acted behind the back of its commander-in-chief, Eoin Mac Neill. When he discovered the plans, only days before they were to be implemented, he was initially tricked into acquiescence. However, on hearing of the loss of the arms, Mac Neill tried to prevent what he now considered a futile and suicidal escapade. As a result, just about ten per cent, of those who the plotters originally hoped to use, participated in the Rising.

The events of Easter Week are sufficiently well known to require little further explanation here, and their portrayal through the medium of postcards is both entirely predictable and somewhat narrow in scope. One can readily observe the absence of humour in cards covering this topic, in contrast, for example, to those relating to Home Rule. Of course, the participants in the earlier crisis were deadly serious, but prior to 1916; people were not dying in Ireland for their beliefs.

With only a few exceptions, cards relevant to these events can be categorised under one of three headings:

Damage caused by the Rising
These cards are mainly, though not exclusively of English/Scottish origin, from major publishers such as Valentine's and Rotary or the *Daily Sketch* newspaper. Hely's of Dublin produced similar material.

Pictures of rebel leaders
These are mainly Irish productions published shortly afterwards by Currans or the Powell Press.

Commemorative/Propagandist
These have been judged of greater relevance to the revival of radical nationalism rather than the Rising itself.

* * * * *

The Revolt of Sinn Feiners in Ireland
Sinn Feiners Parading through the Streets before the Rebellion   4.1

Although the Dublin Castle authorities had their suspicions that some sort of conspiracy was afoot, the planning of the Rising was a reasonably well-guarded secret. One might therefore expect that pictures of republicans prior to the event would be relatively uncommon and this is the case. Drilling was not illegal, but Volunteer marches were sufficiently frequent to attract little attention from either security forces or photographers.

This, (no. 4.1) is one exception, snapped before the outbreak of violence, although the production of the postcard along with its caption obviously happened

The Insurrection in Dublin.—Armoured Motor Car in Bachelor's Walk.   4.2

subsequently. As was the norm at the time in all British sources, the Irish participants in the rebellion were mistakenly referred to as Sinn Féiners.

Scenes of military activity during the Rising were occasionally used on postcards (e.g. no. 4.2), but were far less common than those which depicted the immediate aftermath (e.g. nos. 4.3 to 4.9). Many of the latter concentrated on the damage to the rebel strongholds, and to the centre of Dublin in general. In most cases the pictures speak for themselves and require very little explanation.

A photograph (no. 4.9), showing the Haddington Road/Northumberland Road junction is probably the most interesting of the selection. Some of the fiercest fighting of Easter Week took place in this stretch of road leading towards Mount Street Bridge.

Sherwood Foresters, sent from England to reinforce the Crown Forces, were engaged by rebel snipers for several hours, while they were en route to the centre of the city from the port of Kingstown (Dún Laoghaire). This resulted in the highest casualty for any single incident during the Rising. Of added interest, in this particular case, is the correspondence on the card, referring to the events thus:

> This is the road on which the troops lost several men coming into D(ublin) from Kingstown. Note the bullet marks on corner house.

Some of these are just visible to the naked eye, for example, a cluster on the balustrade, and several just below the roofline on the gable wall, consistent with what one would expect to find, if soldiers were engaged in a firefight with rooftop snipers. A magnifying glass is necessary to reveal further evidence of the gunfire.

4.3

4.4

After the Insurrection.—Interior General Post Office, Dublin.

4.5

5719–12 THE SINN FEIN REVOLT IN DUBLIN. ROTARY PHOTO. E.C.
GENERAL VIEW OF RUINS FROM O'CONNELL BRIDGE.

4.6

After the Insurrection.—
Corner of Bachelor's Walk and Lr. Sackville Street
which commanded O'Connell Bridge.

4.7

Exterior of G.P.O. after Evacuation, showing broken flag-post from which Republican flag was flown.

4.8

4.9

During the course of their revolt, the insurgents sought to publicise their cause with their familiar Proclamation, and the rather less well-known *Irish War News*. The original four page newssheet was issued on the second day of the fighting. This photocopy (no. 4.10), showing the cover of that first and only edition, was published in Britain in postcard form as a curio following the Rising.

The quality of the reproduction was high enough to leave most of the original legible in the postcard copy. Members of the Provisional Government, as they termed themselves, when signing the 1916 Proclamation, can be read on the copy of the back page, with both Patrick Pearse and James Connolly being referred to as 'Commandant Generals'.

The 'Stop Press', which can be followed fairly easily with the aid of slight magnification, is timed at 9:30am Tuesday, 25th April. It describes accurately enough the seizure of the city centre buildings and the attack on Dublin Castle, the seat of the British Administration in Ireland. Nevertheless, the propaganda purpose of the original publication is clearly revealed by its claim: 'the populace of Dublin are plainly with the Republic, and the officers and men are everywhere cheered as they march through the streets.'

Many other contemporary accounts would challenge that assertion. After the rising there is widespread evidence that republican prisoners were jeered and spat at by some of the Dublin inhabitants. At the same time it has to be pointed out that public reactions to the Rising were more complex than is often reported and indeed more research is still required into the matter.

Even the very limited rebel success in taking over a number of key buildings around and within the centre of the city was to prove very short-lived. Static positions for a vastly outnumbered military force do not make any strategic sense. British Army reinforcements soon flooded into Dublin and rebel positions were shelled. The GPO went on fire. The burning of Sackville Street (now O'Connell Street), as a result of the shelling by incendiaries from Trinity College and Parnell Street was also captured on film and produced on a postcard (no. 4.11).

The photographs of the damage to the centre of Dublin, especially the Sackville Street and Eden Quay areas, are not in themselves propagandist, and there is no real evidence that they were intended for use in that fashion. It is true that the sympathies of the *Daily Sketch*, for example, lay firmly with the government, but that is not clear from most of their photographs. With very rare exceptions, the nearest any of these photographic cards from any publisher comes to a judgement is the beautifully ambiguous caption on one card, 'The wreck they made of Church Street.' One obvious exception was a picture of a damaged Liberty Hall under repair, which unlike the standard photos from Hely's, Rotary, *Daily Sketch* and Valentine's depicted a banner on the front with the message 'JAMES CONNOLLY MURDERED MAY 12th 1916.'

However, that is very different from claiming that the destruction shown was not more widely used to spread a propagandist message. That message was spread by advanced nationalists. Novick, in his impressive study, *Conceiving Revolution: Irish Nationalist Propaganda during the First World War*, has pointed out that there was a hiatus in nationalist propaganda in the short-term aftermath of the Rising. His simple but plausible explanation for this was that most of the propagandists were out of circulation. A few were dead, others in hiding, but most were amongst the 1872 prisoners (figures from Foy and Barton's narrative history of the Rising), rounded-up in the days following the rebellion.

The Burning of Sackville Street, Dublin.
(Sinn Fein Rebellion, 1916.)

4.11

Surrender Of P.H. Pearse, April, 29, 1916.

4.12

Traditionally, Irish nationalists have always highlighted the imprisonment of their supporters, and this occasion was no exception. A postcard in the Samuels Collection at Trinity College Dublin, by an anonymous artist shows 'a Corner of Number 3 Dormitory at South Camp Frongoch', part of what was probably the most famous location for Irish prisoners at this time. The pen and ink sketch (not illustrated) seems rather nondescript, but it was obviously considered sufficiently seditious and important at the time to warrant confiscation by the police, and inclusion in the Irish official's private collection. (Arthur Warren Samuels was Irish Solicitor General in 1917, and was appointed Attorney General in 1918.)

Although there were to be numerous later arrests, almost two thirds of these prisoners had been released by Christmas 1916, and there is evidence elsewhere that by then the separatist propagandist machine was back in full working order once again.

Novick gives examples of material on sale by Christmas 1916. He refers to the 'sacrificial' deaths and the 'veritable micro-industry of serious propagandistic commemorative kitsch' which they spawned. The destruction of the city centre was one issue highlighted. The damage was there for all to see. For those not in a position to view it personally, there were the postcards and other written propaganda, such as this extract from A-Z of Current Affairs ,the curriculum supposedly 'Prescribed instead of Irish, 1916–1917, for Teachers under the National Board.'

> Y for New Ypres, which stands on the Liffey,
> By British Huns shelled to the ground in a Jiffy

Pearse offered an unconditional surrender to General Lowe on the afternoon of Saturday 29th April, 'in order to prevent further slaughter of Dublin citizens ...' (no. 4.12). It is difficult to determine the exact number of casualties of the week, but one authoritative source gives them as 230 civilians, 132 crown forces and 64 rebels killed.

Irish Rebellion, May, 1916.

Arrest of Edmund Kent, at 4 a.m.
He was subsequently shot.

4.13

In the eyes of the government, not to mention many Irish people, the rebellion had been a stab in the back, when the country was involved in a major war, and the authorities moved swiftly to seek retribution. By May 3rd, Pearse, McDonagh, and Clarke from amongst the leaders had been court-martialled, sentenced and shot. Further executions followed in rapid succession. This is the context for card no. 4.13, showing the arrest of Edmund Kent (Éamon Ceannt), who had been in command of the rebels in the South Dublin Union, prior to his execution on 8th May.

Ceannt was but one prominent figure of the Rising, who featured on a contemporary postcard. Just about every major figure, and a few minor ones besides, were depicted on the extensive range produced soon after the Rising by the Powell Press in Dublin. Any selection from these is really quite arbitrary. These couple (nos. 4.14 and 4.15) are simply a token sample of what is available.

IRISH REBELLION, MAY 1916.

CORNELIUS COLBERT
(Who took a prominent part in the Rebellion),
Executed May 8th, 1916.

4.14

IRISH REBELLION, MAY 1916

THOMAS ASHE
(Leader of the North County Dublin Volunteers in the Rising),
Sentenced to Death;
Sentence commuted to Penal Servitude for Life.

4.15

Cornelius, better known as Con Colbert, was one of the second rank leaders in 1916. Born in County Limerick in 1886, he grew up to become chief instructor in the republican Boy Scout movement, Fianna Éireann, on its establishment in 1909. The stated aims of that body included the teaching of 'scouting and military exercises, Irish history and the Irish language'. Like many others in this movement, he later joined The Irish Volunteers, and also belonged to the IRB, the secret republican organisation.

During the Rising, Colbert did not initially lead a Volunteer detachment, but he assumed command of a post during the fighting. He was one of the unfortunates, who did not have their sentences commuted to a term of imprisonment. He was shot in Kilmainham during May 1916. At the time of his death he was thirty years of age.

There were no bodies of executed leaders to bury after 1916. There was no scope for 'state' funerals. This undoubtedly enhanced the significance of photographic

4.16

Sinn Fein Rebellion, Dublin   Friends Visiting Sinn Fein Prisoners

4.17

images. Peter Hart, in his study of the IRA has argued that separatist propagandists created a 'patriotic cult' using both the written and pictorial images of the dead leadership of Easter 1916. He believed on the strength of his study of memoirs and of interviews with surviving Old IRA members, that these icons, which were created at this time were 'probably more influential than revolutionary ideas or texts'. Much, although not all, of this imagery was produced in the form of postcards

Amongst those pictured one in particular stands out, namely Thomas Ashe. Thomas Ashe (no. 4.15) was a primary school headmaster and an active member of the Irish Volunteers. He led a group of Volunteers in April 1916, during the most important action of the rebellion outside the city of Dublin. This was the attack on the RIC at Ashbourne, County Meath, as a result of which, eight members of the police, including an Inspector were killed. It is not known if this artist's impression (no. 4.16) gives anything like an accurate representation of the incident. We can be certain, however, that it was not produced as a mere topographical study!

As shown in the caption of no. 4.15, Ashe was amongst those sentenced to death for his role in the violence, but his sentence was quite surprisingly reduced to life imprisonment. Like many other prisoners (no. 4.17), he was released to a hero's welcome in 1917. Thereupon, he resumed his political activity, by helping reorganise the Sinn Féin party.

Thomas Ashe was arrested for incitement under emergency legislation mentioned previously, namely DORA. The prisoners' demands for political status were rejected, and he consequently organised a hunger strike in protest. After a mere few days, Ashe died, as a result of being force-fed. His lying in state and the mass demonstration at his funeral (no. 4.18) certainly contributed to the growing popularity of Sinn Féin (see chapter 5).

THOMAS ASHE FUNERAL, 30th September, 1917—The Firing Party.

4.18

The presentation of these Powell Press cards is very low-key. They all follow a very similar pattern. Under the caption 'Irish Rebellion May 1916,' [sic] is the subject's photograph and name, followed by a phrase giving information about their life or role in the Rising, and finally, a phrase about their subsequent fate, such as 'Executed in Kilmainham Prison May Xth 1916', or 'Sentenced to Death', 'Sentence Commuted to …'.

The matter of fact treatment is probably best explained by commercial realities, namely that this sort of approach was less likely to fall foul of the censor. Certainly to judge from the number of cards viewed from this series, it proved highly popular. In any case, the general tenor of nationalist postcard material following the rising seemed to lay greater emphasis on memorial, sacrifice and martyrdom rather than recrimination. There were of course exceptions such as the following anonymous artist's impression (no. 4.19).

This card is a sequel to another which shows a 1916 execution by firing-squad. In the chosen example, the event is reprised in General Maxwell's nightmare. He had been British C-in-C in Ireland from April to November 1916. He is allegedly haunted, not only by the thoughts of the executions he had organised, using the plenary powers vested in him as Military Governor, but also by the widows or other grieving female relatives of the deceased rebels. In a melodramatic twist, he sleeps or rather attempts to sleep with his revolver by his bedside.

The caption with the phrase 'That Brute Maxwell' quotes from the public and trenchant criticism by Bishop O'Dwyer of Limerick in reply to Maxwell's demand after the Rising that the Bishop discipline some priests in his diocese for their seditious anti-British preaching. It serves to drive home the rather obvious political message. From a factual point of view, this card is a fanciful reconstruction of Maxwell's future life and it reveals nothing that would not be generally known.

NO REST FOR THAT BRUTE MAXWELL!

4.19

Nevertheless, its sentimentality and emotional appeal may add a scintilla to our appreciation of the growing appeal of Sinn Féin in the months and years that followed. Certainly the Bishop became a hero of the separatist movement and both his image and words featured in several contemporary postcards.

And finally, Ireland would not be Ireland if our history were not commemorated and exploited. Most probably, this card (no. 4.20) dates from 1917 or 1918. There is no direct evidence that it is a Sinn Féin production, although its style and content show that it is obviously of that ilk.

Against a backdrop of the GPO in Dublin, from which there radiates a

light to rival the sun, and surrounded by Celtic ornamentation, the four organisations most directly involved in the 1916 Rising are named, namely: the Irish Citizen Army, Oglaigh na hÉireann (Irish Volunteers), Cumann na mBan (female republicans) and Fianna Éireann (Republican Youth).

The medallions displayed prominently on either side of the Post Office carry the Irish harp and the letters 'IV', presumably standing for Irish Volunteers, the largest rebel force during 1916. The commemorative nature of the card is reinforced by the slogan, (borrowed from the song) 'Let Erin Remember'. And Erin did.

4.20

5

THE RISE OF SINN FÉIN 1916–19

Introduction

By 1916 Redmond's influence was already on the wane. Those who had supported the Home Rule policy from 1912 and before had seen no practical benefit. The government was now a wartime coalition with a strong Conservative and Unionist element within it. Redmondites could no longer exploit the balance of power at Westminster as they had from before 1912. The fact that Edward Carson was now Attorney-General would help confirm that Home Rule, as envisaged by Redmond, was a non-runner.

Redmond's other policy of support for the war effort had also turned sour. Initially, Irish business and agriculture had prospered from the War, which many assumed would be of short duration, but now in 1916, those benefits were outweighed by the reality that Irish casualties, like all others, were mounting rapidly with no obvious prospects of success. Who would now give Irish nationalists positive leadership?

Traditionally, the emergence of Sinn Féin as a major political force during 1917 and 1918 has been attributed to a combination of British government blundering and improved nationalist organisation. Undoubtedly, the execution of sixteen participants in the Easter Rising had a traumatic effect on many in Ireland, including many who initially had little or no sympathy with the rebels. The prisoners in British prisons or camps, such as Frongoch, had an opportunity to begin organising an effective movement, a chance, which some readily accepted. Furthermore, on their early release, these former prisoners were frequently treated as heroes.

Extreme nationalists sought to fill the vacuum left by Redmond's decline. Irish contemporaries, just as much as British politicians and press, referred mistakenly to Sinn Féin Volunteers both before and after Easter Week, and these proved an irritant to some of the participants, who had no links whatsoever with that body. Sinn Féin, depending on one's point of view, had been given the credit or blame for the Rising, but it did not immediately emerge, as its propaganda sometimes suggests, phoenix-like from the ashes of 1916. The growth of a new, strengthened party, especially in 1917 was quite complex, but it is not our purpose here to analyse it in any great depth, since the intricacies of its development are not elucidated in postcards of the time.

Nevertheless, two issues in particular, which inspired propaganda, including postcards, seem to have helped Sinn Féin during 1917 and 1918, and those were the death of Ashe after force-feeding on hunger strike, and the proposal to extend conscription to Ireland.

Although the idea of introducing compulsory military service to Ireland had been considered as early as 1916, it was not until April 1918 that it assumed major significance. After the passage of the Military Service Bill, a broad coalition of Irish opinion vehemently denounced the idea. De Valera, President of both the Irish Volunteers and Sinn Féin drew up an anti-conscription pledge, which was loosely modelled on Ulster's Solemn League and Covenant of 1912.

> '… Denying the right of the British Government, to enforce compulsory service in this country, we pledge ourselves solemnly to one another to resist conscription by the most effective means at our disposal.'
>
> (bureauofmilitaryhistory.ie)

Sinn Féin appeared to have gained popularity as the perceived leaders of that campaign, despite the fact that it made up but one element within it. Even the Parliamentary Party opposed conscription, but it would have been the easiest of tasks to target them as hypocrites, given their persistent support since the start of the War for British recruitment in Ireland. The erroneous belief that Sinn Féin constituted the most important resistance to British plans was reinforced by Dublin Castle's discovery, or invention of, 'The German Plot', which was clumsily countered with the arrest of virtually their whole leadership in May 1918.

There can be little doubt that the events outlined here contributed to the growing strength of republicanism, but it would be unwise to suggest that all the more radical nationalists had to do was lie back and profit from the errors of others. Most writers have taken insufficient heed of the impact of Sinn Féin 'propaganda' on Irish public opinion. Admittedly the effectiveness of that particular contribution, some of which came in the form of postcard propaganda, cannot be measured easily. Nevertheless, it should not be ignored.

* * * * *

Postcards reflecting the rise of the independence movement during these years feature certain common themes. They promote Sinn Féin as brave, thorough and forthright in their promotion of Ireland and Irish rights (nos. 5.1 and 5.2). Naturally they portray Britain as hostile or devious or both (no. 5.1). Above all, they attack the Irish Parliamentary Party (nos. 5.3 and following), and sometimes do this rather cleverly. They appear to ignore, or simply do not recognise the unionists. This might seem distinctly odd, but, of course, Sinn Féin saw its struggle for power as being with the Redmondites, and the focus of their attack was designed to undermine the latter by weaning away their support. There was little hope that they could convert a large number of unionists, especially the Ulster unionists.

5.1

The leadership of the Irish Parliamentary Party comes in for particularly strong, personal attack, as in this typical example from 1917 or early 1918 (no. 5.3). It can date from no later since Redmond died in March 1918. Ireland, with her Sinn Féin babe in arms, dismisses little Johnny (John Redmond), who is banished to join his 'foster mother' in England. However, were one to judge from no. 5.4, his reception there was not exactly warm and welcoming.

Under this scenario, as envisaged by another artist, 'recruiting sergeant' Redmond is shown as being rejected by both Ireland and England. He is booted out of his homeland by the new 'Young Ireland,' representing both Irish nationalist tradition and the likes of 'new' Sinn Féin. Demonstrators brandish their placards, 'Fight for Ireland Only', 'Damn the Empire', 'No Recruits For England' and 'Down With Redmond', which represent with a reasonable degree of accuracy a large segment of Irish public opinion after 1916, although it was much more of a minority stance early in the war.

At the same time, Asquith is also shown as dismissing Redmond with disdain. Although the nature of his failure is not stated specifically, it appears pretty obvious that he has failed to supply an adequate contingent of Irish troops to satisfy the British. This issue above all else, with the possible exception of their alleged greed, was the one on which the Redmondites were most consistently attacked.

There can be few more devastatingly scathing insults in the English language than the word 'scab.' This card by Ernest Kavanagh, was also published in Connolly and Larkin's *The Irish Worker* in late 1914 under the caption, 'The One Bright Spot'. It has not been possible to determine when the postcard was issued.

It must represent the ultimate insult for a major political leader to be dismissed with such a term of contempt. He, who has betrayed his own, is now rejected with a withering comment by the new master, whom he has loyally sought to serve.

The allusion to 'Young Ireland' merits particular attention, both as a reference to the past and as a significant factor for the present and near future. The original Young Ireland movement of the early 1840s, under such leaders as Thomas Davis, supported O'Connell's campaign for Repeal of the Act of Union. Later leaders, especially John Mitchel, were not averse to the use of violence, if constitutional means did not succeed. There was a strong parallel between the situations in Irish politics in 1844 and 1917. An appeal to youth was also a feature of the new Sinn Féin's development, and the support of the youthful first-time voters was probably one reason for their success in the election of December 1918. The recently passed Representation of the People Act, gave the vote for the first time to all women over thirty, if

5.2

they were ratepayers or the wives of ratepayers, and to all men over twenty-one except peers, lunatics and felons.

A somewhat similar appeal to the past was also made in no. 5.5, dating from 1915, where the ghost of Wolfe Tone castigates Redmond and Dillon. The father of Irish republicanism condemns the 'traitorous' politicians, who are shown en route to Dublin Castle, the heart of British rule in Ireland.

Greed for 'British Patronage and Gold', forms their alleged motivation. Tone wears his French officer's uniform, in recognition of his achievement in persuading the Directory (i.e. the French republican government) to send expeditions to Ireland in 1796 and 1798. He had in fact been raised to the rank of Adjutant General, prior to the expedition of 1796. The wording of his attack on Redmond and Dillon seems both dated and melodramatic now, but its vehemence could hardly be missed.

Of course Redmond was seen by the republican-minded as being pro-British rather than loyal Irish, because of his support for the war effort since 1914. At the same time one must not forget that these cards are propagandist, and are a distortion of Redmond's true position. Although he loyally supported the war, like most Irishmen in 1914, he had made known his opposition to conscription in Ireland since it was first mooted in 1916.

5.3

Since there are usually no issue numbers or catalogue numbers to assist, many of these cards are extremely difficult to date accurately. Some propagandist material is even known to have been issued on more than one occasion. One cannot even be certain from the pictures themselves (nos. 5.3, 5.4 and 5.5), whether they represent the actual unpopularity of Redmond's moderate policies, or are merely wishful thinking on the part of Sinn Féin. In any case, the decline of the Redmondites was very soon to be a fact of Irish political life. The first hard evidence of this trend came with a series of Sinn Féin by-election victories from 1917. Their sweeping victory (48 per cent of the total vote, 68 per cent of the nationalist vote) in the general election at the end of the following year confirmed it.

5.4

Shade of Wolfe Tone: "Dastards, Traitors, and Felon-Setters." 5.5

The earlier successes are celebrated in no. 5.6, showing the humiliation of Redmond, Dillon, and Devlin. The artist gloats over the 'Sinn Féin' by-election victories in Clare, Longford, Kilkenny and Roscommon. To a greater or lesser extent each of these elections had its own historical significance.

In the North Roscommon election of February 1917, the radicals, or more 'advanced' nationalists, including, but not exclusively Sinn Féin, supported Count Plunkett against the Redmondite candidate. The execution of Plunkett's son Joseph after the Easter Rising no doubt contributed to his victory.

5.6

In South Longford, the National Council, an umbrella body, also including Sinn Féin, selected as its candidate Joseph McGuinness, then a resident of Lewes jail. Use of the prisoner issue with the slogan, 'Put him In to get them Out' was rewarded with a narrow victory for the radicals in May 1917.

Even more dramatic were the events in East Clare. An election became necessary here following the death in action of Major Willie Redmond, younger brother of the party leader. De Valera, the last surviving 'Commandant' from 1916, represented Sinn Féin, and inflicted a sweeping and demoralising defeat on the Redmondites (July 1917).

The *Daily Express* conceded that Sinn Féin had, '… swept the country like a tidal wave …' Although it may not be the case, one would be entitled to wonder if these words were the source of the same cartoonist's inspiration in no. 5.2 and of his very apt caption in no. 5.6.

Finally, the Kilkenny city election had its own share of significance, although it lacked the drama of the Clare election. William Cosgrave, standing as the Sinn Féin candidate, won the seat. He was later to become President of the Dáil, in succession to Arthur Griffith, and later still first 'Prime Minister' of the Irish Free State from 1922 until 1932.

The Sinn Féin movement was obviously growing in strength and their position was further boosted by the death and funeral of Thomas Ashe in September 1917. Novick appeared to assign a pivotal role to the management of the funeral, which both reflected and encouraged a new more aggressive nationalism.

In proposing his thesis Novick compared and contrasted the funerals of Ashe in 1917 and O'Donovan Rossa in 1915. Both funerals were planned and staged. In both cases commemorative programmes, memorial cards, and funeral poetry were issued, but then the differences start to emerge.

The rhetoric and the tone of both differed. Pearse's 1915 speech, 'The fools, the fools, the fools have left us our Fenian dead and while Ireland holds these graves, Ireland unfree will never be at peace', can be seen as threatening but in a vague non-specific sort of way. It could even have been dismissed at the time as empty rhetoric. Novick sums it up beautifully, if possibly a shade too dismissively, 'Once buried, once mourned, O'Donovan Rossa was forgotten.'

The burial of Ashe has a much sharper bite. Armed and uniformed members of the Volunteers and Irish Citizen Army in defiance of new DORA regulations, heard Michael Collins declare, after a volley of shots had been fired over the grave, 'The volley which we have just heard is the only speech which it is proper to make above the grave of a dead Fenian.' One can accept that those words especially after the very real violence of 1916, are much more ominously and aggressively threatening.

He goes on to argue that Ashe unlike O'Donovan Rossa was not forgotten, but that his death inspired practical activities including promotion of the Irish language

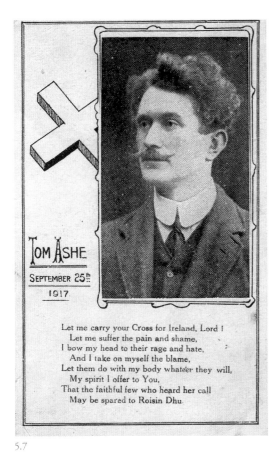

Tom Ashe
SEPTEMBER 25th
1917

Let me carry your Cross for Ireland, Lord !
Let me suffer the pain and shame,
I bow my head to their rage and hate,
And I take on myself the blame,
Let them do with my body whate'er they will,
My spirit I offer to You,
That the faithful few who heard her call
May be spared to Roisin Dhu.

5.7

in honour of Ashe, election fundraising and a generally more violent tone in propaganda. In support of the latter conclusion, he cites a card by Mac Murchadha, entitled 'In His Own Juice', showing Redmond stewing in the cooking pot heated by the fuel of Sinn Féin.

Another card, also located in the Samuels collection, cleverly combines a Sinn Féin 'Doctor' preparing to forcibly feed 'The Right Of Small Nations To Govern Themselves' to a tethered John Bull, and reminding him that he himself had recommended the self-same medicine. It displays a slick reversal of roles, attacking British policy, and at the same time laying out Sinn Féin's most fundamental demand. There may well be a linkage here to the forced feeding of Thomas Ashe, as well as an implied threat of violence in the future, something which has not been encountered in other advanced nationalist cards of this period (see cover).

Likely explanations for the general absence of threats of violence in cards or other media would include the fact that it was never the agreed official policy of Sinn Féin, despite the individual opinions of some of its members, and also that the open encouragement of violence before the general election of December 1918, so soon after the bloodbath of a World War, could have been electorally catastrophic for the Party.

How far, if at all, is Novick's analysis of the effects of Ashe's death, supported by other contemporary postcards? Undoubtedly there is an ample supply of the mourning/commemorative-type card, sometimes combined with verse but as shown here, for example (no. 5.7), it normally falls into the self-sacrificing mode, and the tone is more one of melancholic resignation, rather than anger.

At least one other card has a much more aggressive caption, part of which reads, '… murdered by the English enemy in Mountjoy Prison …' There is also one

THE LAST OF THE SNAKES

5.8

further rare card printed in Germany for Hildesheimer and Co. Ltd., which might lend some support to Novick's interpretation. It shows uniformed Volunteers and a Citizen Army firing party at the funeral (no. 4.18). There is also postcard evidence, including our next example, of aggressive nationalist propaganda directed towards the Parliamentary Party post-September 1917, but there is no obvious linkage in the latter case to Ashe. There may well be plenty of other source material to support Novick's viewpoint, but insufficient evidence could be traced in postcards alone to sustain his argument.

Following the continuing electoral successes for Sinn Féin the same artist now drew an analogy to the legend of St Patrick (no. 5.8). The country's 'saviour of modern times', in the shape of the majestic Sinn Féin eagle once again banishes the snakes, and one could read a lot into that unpleasant representation of the Irish Parliamentary Party. They had failed to deliver Home Rule, and were now in 1918 on the point of virtual extinction by resurgent republicanism.

Throughout this ongoing struggle, Sinn Féin not only cast doubts on their opponents' patriotism, but frequently went further in questioning their whole political motivation (nos 5.8, 5.9 and 5.10). Bernard Partridge had become the chief cartoonist of *Punch* in 1910. Here the Irish artist, Jack Morrow, has borrowed one of his designs to attack an unnamed MP, in all probability, any one of Redmond's Party. The gloating 'Irish Irelander', most likely represents Sinn Féin, although this general term was applied to many of what the British considered the more extreme Irish nationalists, irrespective of whether they were actually members of that party. The first use of the term 'Irish Ireland' is usually attributed to Denis Moran, founder of *The Leader*.

Card no. 5.9, 'Unconquerable,' has an intriguing background, illustrating the work of the propagandist and counter-propagandist. It started life as Partridge's

"UNCONQUERABLE"
WITH APOLOGIES TO BERNARD PARTRIDGE

Irish Irelander. "So, you see—you've lost everything"
Irish M.P. "Not my S— Salary"

5.9

pro-War poster of 1914, subsequently reproduced as a postcard, showing Prince Albert of Belgium standing proudly and defiantly against the German Kaiser despite German atrocities and destruction in his country. The need to fight in defence of Catholic Belgium was one particular recruiting theme used in Ireland.

In 1916, the idea and title were mimicked in an Irish nationalist poster. It showed Patrick Pearse in chains, standing proud and unconquered among the ruins and rubble of Dublin, despite the handing over of his sword to John Bull. In 1917 or 1918 the idea has once again been recycled in our postcard example. The Irish nationalist surrender has in a sense been reversed. Now we have a self-assured Irish Irelander, but

no longer in chains. He stands proud and upright before an effete Irish Parliamentary Party MP, humiliated by the force of 'Irish Public Opinion'. A close study of the card reveals that the Irish Irelander has survived the ruination of Dublin (presumably), and the gallows of 1916.

There can also be no doubt from the Union flag on his jacket, that there is a deliberate attempt to closely associate the Irish Parliamentary Party not with Ireland but with Britain, and all the perceived ills of which she is accused. Now the Irish MP has nothing left but his salary!

The allegedly mercenary nature of Irish Parliamentary Party MPs is also the theme of nos. 5.10 and 5.11. '£400 per year' is a highlight of both

CHORUS OF DILLON & DEVLIN.—"THINK OF THE "PAWTY" JOHN!"

5.10

these examples, a very common motif in the separatist propaganda. That was the annual salary of an MP, since payment was first introduced in 1910. The Sinn Féin propagandist clearly alleges that the Redmondites were at Westminster solely for the money. If that charge were believed in Ireland, then it would severely dent their image.

In the boxing scene, (no. 5.10), Redmond hangs on the ropes, blackened and bruised at the hands of Sinn Féin. This is presumably an allusion to his party's electoral defeats. His seconds, John Dillon and Joe Devlin, urge him to beat the count in their best West Britons' accent, again associating the Party more with Britain than with Ireland. Perhaps only the water bucket and the thought of the £400 can save him. More play is made of this £400 in several other Brewster cartoons not used in this selection.

The subservience and 'true allegiance' of the Party was emphasised in a further example, (no. 5.11) as resplendent with Union Jack, it meekly trots after John Bull. By implication, this is in marked contrast to the independent spirit of Sinn Féin, whose attack on their opponents initially appears more like a bludgeon than a rapier in this instance. However, Novick has suggested a more subtle interpretation, namely that Redmond in this case has been given a Jewish appearance. The author convincingly argues that this postcard may reveal an attempt to associate Redmond with a common anti-Semitic stereotype – the avaricious Jew.

Conspiracy theorists are always with us, but other 'evidence' of anti-Semitism exists in the writings of several of the more active nationalist propagandists, especially Griffith and O'Lonnain. Part of this 'anti-Irish conspiracy' was depicted as an attack on the Catholic religion by Jews and Freemasons, who are sometimes even seen as being synonymous.

This provides the context for the seemingly harmless routine, one could even say boring, photograph of Irish Parliamentary leaders, taken while visiting some of their

French counterparts in 1915. The sting lies in the footnote, probably added some time later. It quotes the French premier, Viviani's attack on religion. Viviani was also a leading Freemason, and reverberations from this meeting were still being felt in 1918 (no. 5.12).

It may be stretching the point too far, but evidence of anti-Semitism in the advanced nationalist propaganda might also be seen in the East London Jewish salesman foisting his inferior goods on the poor Irish in 'Irish Anti-National Exhibition 1907' (no. 1.7).

Both cards (i.e. of the French visit and of the Jewish-looking Redmond)) can be interpreted as an attack on the alleged ineffectiveness of the Parliamentary Party over time, in defending core Irish values, compared to Sinn Féin of course. It is in the same context that we could see Bishop O'Dwyer's earlier attack,

5.12

when he accused the Redmondites of representing 'no opinion Catholic or Irish' (no. 1.5 – 'In The Old Days').

This line of argument has been laboured somewhat, and deliberately so, because of the obvious value of winning clerical support in a deeply religious country. Beyond a shadow of doubt, the Sinn Féin party recognised that fact, and was not slow in exploiting the opportunity.

Finally in softer-coaxing mood, in a complete change of tone from the majority of attacks on their opponents, Sinn Féin pleads with the Parliamentary Party (no. 5.13). If only the Redmondites would cease following the misleading signpost towards the futile Irish Convention, (1917–18), which was boycotted by Sinn Féin; if only they would jettison the millstone of Home Rule, then full Irish independence would be but a short step across the river. The 'one last push' policy must be one of the oldest in the politicians' box of tricks. Jack Morrow also produced a card, now preserved in the Samuels collection, which highlighted the refusal of 'Irish Ireland' to allow themselves to be constrained by participation in the Convention.

IF———

COMPLETE
INDEPENDENCE

HOME RULE

CONVENTION

C.B.

SINN FEIN——" But you can
see yourself, it's only a
stepping-stone to the far side"

5.13

In conclusion, these cards give us a clear enough idea of what the radicals opposed. As it were, they give us a clear common denominator. However, they have severe limitations in elucidating the internal debate and even dissension within their movement. Apart from claiming Irish independence, they do not reveal much about what their supporters stood for, but there is good reason for that omission.

All the radicals were dissatisfied with the policy of Home Rule, which was by then not really on offer anyhow, at least as originally proposed in 1912. They were opposed to attendance at Westminster, and they all seemed to agree with the policy of making Ireland's case internationally at the Peace Conference, whenever the War would end. Beyond that, they seemed uncertain. A modern historian described Sinn Féin as late as 1918 as 'rambling and amorphous'. Lee's description of their policy in 1917 and 1918 as 'studiously vague' (p. 41), also seems particularly apt.

Probably the most revealing observation which can be made about these cards is not so much about what they contain but what they omit.

Arthur Griffith T.D.

5.14

Numerous cards use words or phrases like 'freedom', 'the will of the people', 'independence', and 'the right of small nations to govern themselves'. It is dangerous to claim that the word 'republic' never appears in any of these cards, but it has not been observed in a single one. Perhaps the term 'republic' was too nebulous for the proverbial man in the street, and the slogan 'The Will of the People' was more easily understood and therefore more likely to benefit Sinn Féin electorally.

One other possible explanation for its intriguing omission could be that support for a republic, even amongst the advanced nationalists, despite the Proclamation in 1916, was not yet unanimous, although it was to become clearly-defined Sinn Féin policy at the Ard-Fheis of October 1917. Central to the internal divisions as late as the

5.15

summer of 1917, was Arthur Griffith (no. 5.14). He argued, ultimately without success, for a less than totally independent Irish state, on the premise that retaining links with Britain stood a better chance of placating Ulster unionists. He was one of the few who appears to have taken them seriously. He also remained uncomfortable with the idea that violence would possibly be used to establish a republic.

Like Griffith, Fr Michael O'Flanagan (no. 5.15) was Vice-President of Sinn Féin. He had come to prominence through land agitation in County Roscommon, Plunkett's Liberty League, and the National Council, which tried to coordinate radical nationalist groupings and resolve internal differences. Like Griffith he was unhappy about the use of violence, and even went as far as to unilaterally contact Lloyd George in 1920 to seek peace, a policy, which the majority of Sinn Féin rejected at that time.

However, none of these nuances of policy have been examined in this study, since it has proved impossible to trace them in postcards, and it is probably unreasonable to expect that they would be found. In any case, it was the men of violence who gained the upper hand and seized the initiative.

The rationalisation for their violent actions was the rejection by the international community in general, and Britain in particular of their claim to independence, i.e. full Irish self-determination, as they understood that term. Their claim is shown

PAT–"I just want the same full measure as my friend here!"

5.16

in documentary form referred to elsewhere, in postcards such as no. 5.16, which compares Ireland unfavourably to the newly constructed independent state of *Jugoslavia*, in cards such as 'UP PLUNKETT' (no. 3.16), and in several others not reproduced here. (There has to be a certain irony in this separatist cartoonist's image of Pat's demand for the 'full measure' as it re-echoes a very similar Fitzpatrick cartoon from 1906, in which Redmond was shown rejecting the half-measure of Devolution in place of the full measure of Home Rule.)

It is the activities of these men of violence, which we will now examine, in so far as they were shown in postcards of the time.

6

VIOLENCE 1919–23

Introduction

Following their victory in the recent general election of December 1918, the successful Sinn Féin candidates refused to attend Westminster. This was in accordance with the first clause of their Election Manifesto. In it they pledged to establish the Irish Republic:

> By withdrawing the Irish Representation from the British Parliament and by denying the right and opposing the will of the British or any other foreign Government to legislate for Ireland.

Instead of taking their seats in parliament some 28 Sinn Féiners assembled in Dublin to establish their alternative assembly. On that same day, 21st January 1919, coincidentally, in so far as we can tell, members of the Irish Volunteers, soon to be more commonly known in Ireland as the IRA, attacked and killed two RIC men who were escorting a cartload of gelignite at Soloheadbeg, County Tipperary.

This shooting incident marked the start of the 'Troubles', also referred to as the Anglo-Irish War or the War of Independence. The main protagonists were the IRA, on the one side, and the RIC, later augmented by the Black and Tans and the Auxiliaries on the other. Regular British troops were also active but on many occasions, did not play the major role, presumably, because their government considered the Irish violence a policing rather than a military problem. To have acted otherwise, could have added credence to the IRA claim to be an Army engaged in a liberation campaign. Lloyd George, at least, was determined to resist that. The IRA nominally accepted the authority of the Irish parliament, i.e. the Dáil, on whose behalf they were allegedly fighting, but in practice they were largely anarchic.

From January 1919 until early 1920, IRA violence was sporadic, consisting mainly of arms raids on isolated police stations and attacks on individual members of the RIC, more than 50 of whom were murdered in the first six months of 1920 alone. After the first year, violence escalated. More frequent ambushes, shootings and government reprisals, which will not be detailed here, continued throughout the year until a Truce was called in July 1921. Protracted negotiations came to a conclusion with the Articles of Agreement, more commonly known as the 'Treaty', in December. Because this agreement offered Dominion status to the Irish Free State rather than full independence, and because of other conditions attached, it became the subject of heated debate in the Dáil, before it was eventually accepted by the narrow majority of sixty-four to fifty-seven.

Divisions between Irish nationalist politicians, and within the IRA, over this issue deepened and then developed by June 1922 into a Civil War. Following what was unofficially called 'the Second Battle of O'Connell Street,' (the Easter Rising being the first), the anti-Treaty Republicans (Irregulars) were driven out of their strongholds in central Dublin after almost a fortnight's fighting. Some spasmodic fighting continued in Dublin for a few weeks but, after losing their hold on the city centre, they then tried to concentrate their strength in the southern half of the country in what they declared 'the Munster Republic,' until eventually they were forced to concede defeat by May the following year. Amongst the prominent casualties of this violence were Michael Collins and Liam Lynch, Chief-of-Staff of the Irregulars.

Although material on this period is relatively scarce, a certain amount has survived, including several pictures of the Dáil, at least one cartoon, pictures of participants in political negotiations, and memorial cards for some of those killed. A certain amount of photographic material of the Civil War also exists in postcard form, of which a number of scenes captured on film by W.D. Hogan are best known.

* * * * *

An imaginary scene from the House of Commons at Westminster graphically reflects the political situation in Ireland during the early part of 1919. We are shown row upon row of vacant benches, as the Prime Minister, Lloyd George, makes his address from the dispatch box in grand oratorical style (no. 6.1).

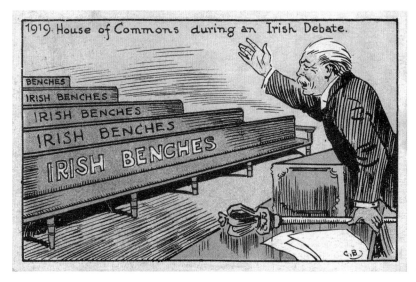

6.1

6.2

DAIL EIREANN, AN CHEAD TIONOL, 21 EANAIR, 1919.
Sreath 1.—(i dtosach)—S. O'Dochartaigh, S. O. hAodha, S. O'Ceallaigh, Conte Pluingcéad, C. Brugha, S. T. O'Ceallaigh,
P. O'Maille, S. Breathnach, T. O'Ceallaigh.   Sreath 2.—S. MacSuibhne, C. O. hUigin, D. O'Buachala, E. O'Dubhgain,
P. Béaslaoi, An Dr. O'Riain, An Dr. O'Cruadhlaoigh, P. Mac an Bhaird, P. O'Maoldomhnaigh, R. Suataman.   Sreath 3—
R. Bartuin, R. O'Maolchatha, C. O'Coileain, P. O'Seanachain, S. de Burca.

While the picture is perfectly clear, its political viewpoint is not immediately apparent, leaving some room for differences in interpretation. It may simply be saying that Lloyd George has nothing relevant or worthwhile to say to Irish MPs.

Alternatively it may also be asserting that Irish politicians do not like his message. Since the presumed artist of this piece, Gordon Brewster also produced propaganda promoting Sinn Féin, the probability must be that he refers here to that Party's boycott of Westminster. With a little artistic licence, the Irish benches are shown completely empty.

The picture is reminiscent of an earlier *Punch* cartoon by T.H. Townsend showing the Irish Chief Secretary, Augustine Birrell, talking about Home Rule to an empty Commons. The message then was that the real action, as it were, was taking place outside parliament. Here the message is taken to be similar.

Sinn Féin had gained 73 of the 105 Irish seats in the December 1918 election. Those members, not in prison, had assembled the following month on 21st January in Dublin's Mansion House to establish the First Dáil, as the parliament of the Republic, to which they pledged their allegiance (no. 6.2). The official record of that first meeting declared with a certain bravado that the absentees were 'fe ghlas ag Gallaibh' – imprisoned by foreigners.

No. 6.3 shows the second session, dated April 10th, of this same body in the same location. Like no. 6.2, it gives the names of all the deputies in Irish. The captions, likewise in Irish emphasise Sinn Féin's commitment to the language.

Although official group photographs like these do not have a great deal of instant appeal, it would be rash to hastily dismiss their historical importance. Between them, these cards present us with images of most of nationalist Ireland's key political figures of the time.

DAIL EIREANN, AN TARNA TIONOL, 10 ABRAN, 1919.

Sreath 1.—(i dtosach)—L. MacFhionnghail, M. O'Coileain, C. Brugha, A. O'Griobhtha, E. de Bhailera, S. Conte Pluingcéad, E. MacNeill, L. MacCosgair, E. de Blaghd. Sreath 2.—P. O'Maoldhomhnaigh, T. MacSuibhne, R. O'Maolchatha, S. O'Dochartaigh, S. O'Mathghamhna, S. O'Deolain, S. MacAonghusa, P. O'Caoimh, M. MacStain, S. MacCraith, An Dr. B. O'Ciosog, L. de Roiste, L. Colibhet, An tA. M. O'Flannagain. Sreath 3.—P. Mac an Bhaird, A. MacCaba, D. MacGearailt, S. MacSuibhne, An Dr. R. O hAodha, C. O'Coileain, P. O'Maille, S. O'Meadhra, B. O hUigin, S. de Burca, C. O hUigin. Sreath 4.—S. MacDonnchadha, S. Mac an tSaoi. Sreath 5.—P. Beaslaoi, R. Bartuin, P. O'Gallagain, Sreath 6.—P. O'Seanachain, S. Etchingham.

6.3

The first meeting, coinciding with the first violence of the War of Independence, shows 24 of those present, while the April photograph contains 41. One notable addition in the later example is Eamon de Valera (centre row 1). His appearance was possible following his escape from Lincoln Jail in February 1919. In April, at this second assembly, he assumed the Presidency of the Dáil from Cathal Brugha (pictured third from left, row 1 between Michael Collins and Arthur Griffith).

One of the more colourful incidents of 1919 was that known as 'The Limerick Soviet'. The local military authorities had panicked somewhat in response to a shooting incident at the Limerick Workhouse Hospital. In April 1919, an RIC guard and a republican prisoner, Bobby Byrne, died of gunshot wounds, received in the course of a failed rescue attempt. His funeral was attended by an estimated 15,000 people (no. 6.4). The military authorities in Limerick declared martial law, fearing that the incident was the start of a major insurgency.

In response, the Limerick United Trades and Labour Council, representing some 35 unions called a general strike. Strike committees organised permits, food supplies and a strike news-sheet, but the whole affair lasted less than a fortnight. After appeals from the local bishop and from employers, plus negotiations with the military authorities, a return to normal work was declared.

The 'Soviet' is indicative of both the power and limitations of the press. They gave it its name and it stuck. There was no real workers' control, but the use of the term is indicative of the spirit of the times, occurring as it did contemporaneously with the Allied Intervention against the Reds in Russia, the Munich Soviet and Bela Kun's short-lived Communist takeover in Hungary.

6.4

Limerick City Museum holds a fairly extensive collection of ephemera dealing with 'the Soviet', including four locally produced postcards of Byrne's funeral, and a single example of an army roadblock on one of the bridges across the Shannon. They are interesting illustrations, but unfortunately do not illuminate or analyse the event to any great extent, although the roadblocks appear from contemporary written sources to have been a particular source of grievance for some workers, as they created major problems for them in getting to and from work.

Having faced almost a year of violence throughout 1919, the RIC started to withdraw from barracks in outlying districts, since they were proving especially vulnerable to attack. As a consequence, law and order was breaking down especially in the south and south-west of the country. The government at Westminster now attempted to stiffen police morale by sending police reinforcements, namely, the Black and Tans, the first group of which arrived in Ireland in the spring of 1920. They were supported later in the year by the Auxiliaries.

This new development figured as the subject of a card by Art Kavanagh (no. 6.5). While the artwork may not merit much attention, the message is of interest. A Black and Tan is shown in the company of an RIC man, and his travel plans are being subtly thwarted by an uncooperative engine-driver. From the field-gun and the other Black and Tans, just visible in the top left-hand corner, it seems plain that the driver is quietly sabotaging the plans of a British convoy. Since they had quickly become both hated and feared, putting one over the Tans in this fashion through passive resistance would have proved immensely popular amongst Irish nationalists. We know from other research that railway workers refused to handle military

95

IRISH ENGINE DRIVER—
" STEAM IS OFF, BLACK AND TAN.
NOTHIN' DOIN'."

6.5

materials during 1920 (see Townsend in *Irish Historical Studies* vol. 21 no. 83, 1979).

Postcards can reveal something about political attitudes, but where they fall down is in the depiction of war in all its horror. Leaving aside all thoughts of propaganda for the moment, the reality of killing is most unlikely to be portrayed. One must not forget that postcards were a commodity, for sale in the marketplace. A blood and guts approach was unlikely to appeal to many on any level, irrespective of their political sympathies. To some extent war has to be romanticised and it certainly has to be sanitised for public consumption. Nevertheless, we do get a glimpse of the suffering though a very one-sided view, through commemorative pictures of republican casualties in postcard form.

Amongst the more memorable is this category is a memorial card issued in Glasgow following the death of Terence MacSwiney (no. 6.6). A member of the Irish Volunteers and Sinn Féin, MacSwiney was elected to the First Dáil as a representative of Mid-Cork. (See also no. 6.3 in this chapter, row 2, second from the left). When Tomás Mac Curtain, IRA Commandant and Lord Mayor of Cork, was shot dead in March 1920, allegedly by the RIC, MacSwiney succeeded him as First Citizen.

When MacSwiney himself was arrested in August under the emergency legislation for 'being in possession of documents the publication of which

Terence MacSwiney - Lord Mayor of Cork,
Died in Brixton Prison, 25th. October 1920.

6.6

would be likely to cause disaffection to His Majesty', he immediately went on hunger-strike. Because he was popular in Cork and a high profile prisoner he was removed from his power base to prison in England. From a propaganda point of view this was counter-productive for the government. MacSwiney persisted in his hunger-strike for seventy-four days before dying on the morning of 25th October 1920 in a welter of publicity.

The *Daily Telegraph*, a publication never noted for its republican sympathies, observed (as quoted in Bennett, p. 90):

> The Lord Mayor of Cork condemned himself to death for the sake of a cause in which he passionately believed, and it is impossible for men of decent instincts to think of such an act unmoved.

His funeral was likely to become an occasion of mass demonstration in Ireland. It was somewhat muted, however, when the military authorities, aware of the possible propaganda value of the funeral for Sinn Féin, having learnt from the funerals of Ashe and to a lesser extent Byrne, shipped the body directly to Cork from England, contrary to republican plans for the cortege to travel by road from Dublin to Cork.

Less than a month after the MacSwiney funeral, one of the best known and most gruesome incidents of the war occurred, commonly referred to as Bloody Sunday (21st November 1920). Following the shooting on that single day of twenty nine people, fourteen of them British agents, the authorities carried out a series of arrests. Amongst those charged with one of the killings was Thomas Whelan from Clifden, Connemara. The *Irish Times* reported:

> Thomas Whelan was tried by court-martial at the City Hall, Dublin charged with the murder of Captain Bagallay, at Baggot Street Dublin on the 21st November, there being an alternative charge of manslaughter.

Although his three co-defendants were all acquitted, Whelan was convicted of murder. Despite widespread appeals for clemency, and questions in the Westminster parliament, the Crown prerogative of mercy was refused and Whelan was hanged in Mountjoy Prison on 14th March 1921. It was one of six executions carried out on that same day, a quarter of the number officially put to death by the British during these Troubles (no. 6.7).

This rare photograph shows Whelan flanked by an RIC man and a Black and Tan, in what appears to be the exercise-yard of Mountjoy. Curiously the prisoner does not seem to be overly concerned about his plight.

Without knowing the exact circumstances under which this photograph was taken, it is difficult to explain the prisoner's apparent good humour. Perhaps this was taken before sentencing. Perhaps what looks like a smile is simply a nervous

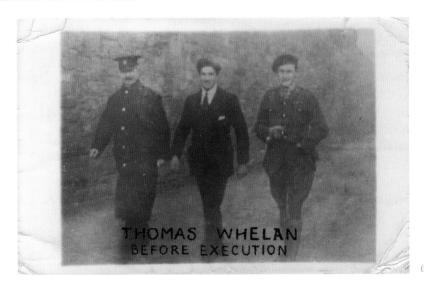

THOMAS WHELAN
BEFORE EXECUTION

6.7

grimace or perhaps, the *Irish Times* report might suggest another not entirely convincing explanation:

> He was seen in Mountjoy Prison on Saturday (12th March) by his mother, who told a Press representative that her son was bright happy and cheerful. He denied all knowledge of the murder and told his mother that if all were as happy as he was she would not worry very much.

> 'It is well known,' he said 'that I am innocent, and had no knowledge, hand act or part in the tragedies of 21st November, and I am reconciled to my fate, and am prepared to meet my God.'

As well as the official executions, there were a considerable number of even more controversial killings and unexplained arson attacks, for which Crown forces were responsible. Even at this distance in time, it is often impossible to say whether they were official state reprisals, unofficial local actions with which some authorities colluded, or simply unofficial actions for which the political and security authorities considered it wiser not to admit responsibility. Particularly notable of the former was the burning of Cork city centre in December 1920, also featuring in postcards of the time (but not illustrated here.) Of the latter, most noteworthy were the 'Curfew Murders', which occurred just a week prior to the multiple executions in Mountjoy.

Within half an hour of each other, the republican mayor and ex-mayor of Limerick, George Clancy and Michael O'Callaghan, were shot dead at their homes by visiting gunmen in the early hours of 7th March 1921. Names of the alleged gunmen have been bandied about, but unsurprisingly nothing has been proven. A considerable amount was written about the killings at the time and a single postcard exists in Limerick City Museum, a photograph of George Clancy in Irish dance costume, a title in Gaelic which translates as 'who was murdered by the British 7th March 1921' and a Gaelic verse as a eulogy for the deceased (not illustrated).

In the first instance, this is a memorial card for a prominent murder victim. However, one could also categorise it as similar to the Powell Press photographs of the 1916 leaders. The use of the Irish language is not surprising, given the victim's longstanding commitment to it, and it was a cause supported by quite a number of his associates. It may,

JOHN DOYLE
GAVE HIS LIFE FOR IRELAND
Shot in action, Custom House, May 1921.

6.8

however, have limited the card's possible value as propaganda since fewer would have understood the inscriptions. It may also of course have helped it to escape the censor!

It would be difficult, probably impossible to narrate a detailed chronological account of all the violence through postcards alone. There were notable exceptions, but most of the conflict consisted of ambushes involving relatively small numbers of combatants. One of those exceptions and one of the last major incidents of the Anglo-Irish War was the attack on the Dublin Custom House on 25th May 1921, aimed at crippling the British administration. It was an important propaganda symbol of British rule in Ireland, but not important enough to be properly guarded! The building was set on fire. Tax files and the records of Local Government Boards were burnt. Tim Pat Coogan summed it up neatly as, 'a publicity success and a military debacle'. This incident was not typical, as it came close to becoming the sort of battle in which the IRA could not afford to become engaged.

One expert claimed that several hundred were involved. In the ensuing gun battle with the Auxiliaries, dozens of IRA men were captured, several were wounded, and five were shot dead. Card no. 6.8 commemorated one of these. Its political sympathies are obvious.

The IRA could not sustain losses of this magnitude over an extended period but the British government too faced its problems. There was internal dissension over its tactics. There was embarrassing questioning from America and criticism from

John Bull:—"I'd like to, but———!"

6.9

its own press. If they condoned reprisals and a more draconian security policy, they faced further problems. Alternatively, if they appeared too lenient they met with other hawkish criticism. This dilemma and the caption have a certain timelessness about them, which was well-illustrated in another contemporary card (no. 6.9). The picture and caption are largely self-explanatory.

This cartoon highlights a pretty-well-universal dilemma through the ages, for democratic governments at least. They obviously feel the need to respond robustly to any sort of violent or terrorist threat. However, today's over-reaction may well serve the development of tomorrow's terrorist.

IRISH PEACE CONFERENCE, JULY, 1921.   Gathering at the Mansion House.
E. & S. Ltd., Dublin]   [Photo, Hogan, Dublin

6.10

IRISH PEACE CONFERENCE, JULY, 1921. [General Macready entering Mansion House with Lord Mayor.
E. & S. Ltd., Dublin]   [Photo, Hogan, Dublin   6.11

Given the growing war-weariness of both sides, it is not surprising that attempts were made to end the deadlock by negotiations. This picture of a gathering at Dublin's Mansion House records the effective end of the War of Independence (no. 6.10). Another in the same quite extensive series issued by Eason's of Dublin shows the arrival of General Macready, GOC British Forces in Ireland for a meeting with IRA leaders, which resulted in a Truce coming into effect on 11th July 1921 (no. 6.11). A few days later De Valera led a delegation to Downing Street to meet Lloyd George for an initial discussion on peace proposals, while much of Ireland held its breath (no. 6.12).

Irish Peace Conference, July, 1921.   Deputation from Irish Cities awaiting arrival of Delegates from England with Peace Proposals.
Left to right—H. O'Friel (Dublin Co. Council) ; Mrs. O'Donovan (Deputy Mayor of Limerick); Dr. Vincent J. White, T.D. (Mayor of Waterford);
Mrs. O'Callaghan (Widow of Late Mayor of Limerick); Donal O'Callaghan, T.D. (Lord Mayor of Cork); Liam De Roiste, T.D. (Cork).
                                                                                                                             6.12

GENERAL ELECTION

ORGANISATION

G.B.

THE GUN TO WIN THE DAY

6.13

Although the Anglo-Irish War was ended, peace was still elusive, as sectarian violence not only continued but intensified within Northern Ireland, where it lasted until the summer of 1922, and Civil War was just over the horizon for the rest of the island.

After tortuous negotiations, terms of a treaty were agreed between British and Irish delegations in December. These proposals opened deep divisions within the republican movement. Dissension simmered for some months until in April 1922, republicans opposed to the Treaty, which the politicians had narrowly accepted, seized control of the Four Courts building, the centre of the judiciary in Ireland.

Despite this and other provocations, there was a reluctance to start a civil war. A 'Peace Committee' of prominent Pro- and Anti-Treaty figures met several times during April and May but failed to find a resolution to the fundamental disagreement. Consequently, Collins and De Valera agreed a rather odd electoral pact in May 1922. It envisaged a sort of pro-rata power-sharing between Pro- and Anti- Treaty Sinn Féin. The election of June showed majority support for the former, but unsurprisingly it also solved nothing.

This was the context for another Brewster card (no. 6.13). He depicts the false hope of the election with the rather clichéd image of the rising sun. Now that the election has failed to solve the problem, the better organised Free Staters will resort to the gun. Since we do not have an exact issue date for the card we cannot determine whether Brewster was being prescient, or if his card is simply a common sense comment after the election. The false dawn of the general election is to be replaced by the harsh reality of organisation for warfare.

After some brief further hesitation, the Provisional Government of the Free State set up under the Treaty, and now under pressure from the British to show its

6.14

E. & S., Ltd., D.]   **Military Operations, Dublin, June–July, 1922.**   [Photo, Hogan, Dublin.
SHELL EXPLODING ON FOUR COURTS.

authority, used its newly formed army with artillery support to drive the anti-Treaty forces out of the Four Courts.

This is traditionally seen as the opening salvo of the Irish Civil War (1922–23). It is probably its best known image, seen in rare film footage as well as in postcard form (no. 6.14). Another card from the same time, whether real or staged, recorded a scene at a barricade (no. 6.15), (during a lull in the shooting, one assumes since the soldier on the right presented himself as a very large target,) in the 'Second Battle of O'Connell Street'. Since the anti-Treaty Irregulars often wore no military uniforms, they were not readily identified. For this reason, the Free State Army,

E. & S., Ltd. ₃D]   **Military Operations, Dublin, June–July. 1922.**   [Photo. Hogan, Dublin.
NATIONAL ARMY RESERVES AT BARRICADE.   6.15

r.. & S., Ltd., D.]   Military Operations, Dublin, June–July, 1922.   [Photo, Hogan, Dublin.
NATIONAL TROOPS SEARCHING CIVILIANS.   6.16

now calling itself the National Army as some of the cards indicate, conducted regular searches of civilians (no. 6.16). It appears to have been an everyday occurrence. In a confirmation of this, a contemporary observation, albeit a rather biased one in *The Workers Republic*, official organ of the Communist Party of Ireland on the 12th August 1922 noted in a droll comment, 'To be suddenly surrounded and searched on the street is as commonplace as taking one's breakfast.'

On first impressions, this additional picture, no. 6.17, could so easily be dismissed as just another building damaged in the conflict. However, it is of greater significance than might at first be imagined. Having escaped from the bombardment of the Four Courts, Cathal Brugha, former President of the Dáil, took up position in the Hamman Hotel shown here. (*The Directory of Dublin* 1920 listed 'The Hammam [sic] family hotel and Turkish Baths, at nos. 11–13 Sackville Street Upper, i.e. O Connell Street). This building in turn, came under heavy fire from the Free State forces. Rather than flee or

E. & S., Ltd., D.]   Military Operations, Dublin, June–July, 1922.   [Photo, Hogan, D.
NATIONAL FORCES BOMBING HAMMAM HOTEL.

6.17

surrender, Brugha advanced from the hotel, gun (or guns) in hand, and was fatally wounded. He was one of the most prominent casualties on the anti-Treaty side. Other Hogan pictures used in this series of cards show some of the damage to the centre of Dublin after the defeat of the Irregulars in the city.

After their defeat in Dublin, the Irregulars retreated southwards and declared the Munster Republic. Lee refers to the 'key struggle around Limerick' and this was reflected in at least three postcards in the Eason's series, with the heading 'Siege of Limerick July 1922'. One shows Free State barricades in O'Connell Street, while a second shows 'Danny Boy' the Free State armoured car, which was used to strafe Irregular positions in the town centre.

Irregulars had occupied barracks evacuated by the British and RIC. (These included the former House of Industry, a voluntary Workhouse and Infirmary set up in the 1770s before a state system was established. Later it became Strand Barracks). The Irregulars' static positions, similar to both 1916 and their more recent defeat in Dublin left them as 'sitting ducks'. Free State troops took up positions and in a microcosm of the Four Courts attack deployed an 18 pounder artillery piece against Strand Barracks on 20th July. Two shells only were fired, one of them piercing the barrack's perimeter wall (no. 6.18). This seems to have been sufficient to sap the morale of the defenders, because in the early hours of the following morning, they set fire to the other barracks which they held, and began a further retreat southwards to continue their struggle in some of the surrounding villages. The importance of the loss of Limerick would seem to be confirmed by the fact that within three weeks the Anti-Treaty forces had lost control of every urban area in Ireland.

E. & S., Ltd., D.]   Siege of Limerick, July, 1922.   [Photo, Hogan, Dublin.
BREACH MADE IN STRAND BARRACKS BY ARTILLERY.   6.18

E. & S., Ltd., D.   Funeral of the late General Collins, August 28th, 1922.   [Photo. Hogan, Dublin.
                          REMOVING BODY FROM PRO-CATHEDRAL.   6.19

These cards clearly have their limitations but they constitute an interesting pictorial record of an important event and are at least indicative of the superior firepower of the Free State Army.

Of the nine hundred or so who died in this vicious struggle, the most distinguished victim on the government side was Michael Collins, (no. 6.19), Chairman of the Provisional Government and Commander-in-Chief of the Free State Army. During a tour of inspection of his forces, he was killed in an ambush at Beal na mBlath, County Cork in August 1922.

By the time of Collin's death, the tide of war was flowing strongly in favour of the Free State, although the Irregulars remained unwilling to accept defeat. After his death, it continued with escalating bitterness, not reflected in contemporary postcards. Government forces drove home their advantage with ruthless efficiency, and the anti-Treaty IRA were soon reduced to militarily ineffective sniping, until April 1923, when they were forced to recognise the futility of further resistance.

In total, between 1919 and 1923, about 2,750 people met violent deaths. Just under a quarter of all the victims were police or other Crown forces. It has to be conceded that postcard coverage of these events gives us a quite incomplete picture. Memorials of republicans are fairly scarce but not all that rare, while virtually none of British or RIC victims could be traced. Although a few cards showing IRA units in training are known to exist, there are very few 'action shots.' Given the nature of guerrilla campaigns such as the Anglo-Irish War or most of the Civil War that should not really be surprising. The sectarian violence in Northern Ireland, which took place more or less concurrently, and which left over 400 dead, seems to have gone unrecorded in postcard form.

7

NORTHERN IRELAND

Introduction

In Britain, the 'Golden Age' of postcards is generally considered to have ended by the early 1920s. As far as Irish political cards were concerned, the issue of Civil War cards seems to mark the end of their popularity in the south. In the north, very little was produced in the half-century following the Home Rule Crisis.

Some exceptions do exist, nevertheless, for example, a series of photographs depicting crowds and leading personalities in June 1921, before, during and immediately after the state opening by George V of the Northern Ireland Parliament in Belfast City Hall. One might also have expected some 'editorial comment' in postcard form for or against the specific issue of partition. It does not appear to exist. The closest relevant material came from July 1917 in two cartoons (not shown) by Jack Morrow, whose work was often issued as postcards, but it could not be confirmed if these two examples from the paper *New Ireland* were amongst them.

One could also reasonably expect to see some photographic record in postcard form of the 1920–22 'Northern Troubles', but it does not appear to exist either, with the exception of a posed photograph of B Specials from around 1920, which could only be considered of peripheral relevance. On the other hand, the dearth of material during much of this period can hardly be surprising. With the establishment of Northern Ireland, unionists no longer had any great need to campaign. Nationalists were embittered, and in many cases, even despairing and disillusioned after their political defeat. Staunton in his study of Northern Ireland nationalism makes this point time and time again.

Nationalists had no great cause in which they could have realistic hopes. Consequently, politics in the 1920s and 1930s was a fairly dull affair. Neither Licensing nor Education Acts, for example, could be considered very photogenic, would scarcely engender propaganda, and would have held out little prospect of profit for a postcard publisher.

With the rare exceptions of a couple of cartoons from the 1920s, a handful of examples from 1934, election promotional material, a passing reference to the Second World War, and a single card from 1966, very little else of note could be found, until the outbreak of the most recent 'Troubles' in the 1960s led to another upsurge of postcard production.

While loyalists and nationalists would give sharply different explanations, they would certainly agree that Northern Ireland's relatively short history has been punctuated by outbreaks of sectarian conflict. This is reflected to some degree in the range of postcards issued, the vast majority of which were produced in the last twenty-five years or so. While they promote both republican and unionist viewpoints, there is little doubt that republican propagandists, or at least those sympathetic to their cause, have dominated the more recent production of postcards.

A sizeable portion of those modern cards, which originated from loyalist groups, consisted of mere replicas of earlier examples from the 1912 Home Rule Crisis (e.g. nos 7.16–18). By way of exception, some loyalist paramilitary organisations also reproduced the work of wall artists in the form of postcards, (nos. 7.14 and 7.19 for example). A similar range showing copies of murals from nationalist areas also exists, and both apparently have considerable appeal for foreign tourists.

* * * * *

The Government of Ireland Act, 1920, marked another attempt by the British government to solve the Irish Question. The working out of that policy is shown here in one of several cards showing the official opening of the Northern Ireland Parliament, with the subsequent installation of James Craig as Prime Minister. In some respects, however, the most interesting figure in this photograph is the somewhat less well-known Lieutenant-Colonel Wilfrid Spender (no. 7.1).

As an ex-army Captain of firmly held unionist sympathies, Spender was invited to Ulster in 1913, by the Unionist leader, Edward Carson. He was appointed Assistant Quartermaster General of the recently formed UVF. As one of the small committee intimately involved in the planning of the Larne gun-running, he was

Hurst & Co., Belfast.

State Opening of Northern Parliament by the King and Queen, 22nd June, 1921.
SIR JAMES CRAIG, HIS SON AND LT -COL. SPENDER.

7.1

present at Larne in April 1914, under the command of Sir William Adair, but his role in Ulster affairs did not end there.

In July 1920, Spender had been given command of the revived UVF, with 'Lloyd George's tacit approval'. However, General Macready, the army commander-in-chief in Ireland, was less than happy with this development. Accordingly, in November 1920, apparently at Spender's suggestion, the British government was persuaded to fund a new force, the USC or Ulster Special Constabulary. The Northern Ireland government recruited an armed force of some 20,000 men to support the newly formed RUC. As the architect of this new force, Spender probably deserves a greater prominence than he has sometimes been given in the hierarchy of unionist figures.

Several other pictures of Sir James Craig are known to exist in postcard form but they are not numerous. With one exception (Lord Londonderry) efforts to find images of other members of his government were unsuccessful.

Sinn Féin boycotted the Northern Ireland Parliament, so one would not expect to see much of them. Other nationalists attended fitfully. Joseph Devlin seems to have been the only one of these to come to the attention of postcard publishers. Here, in no. 7.2, and in other cards he is singled out for attack.

Like the Archangel Gabriel, who summons the dead from the grave, 'Wee Joe', calls on the deceased, who rise protesting from their graves – and not for the first time! They form his 'Reserve Voters', who are drafted into service to ensure a nationalist victory in the traditionally hard-fought West Belfast constituency.

Although it is an open secret that personation was, and allegedly remained until very recently, a regular even traditional feature of most Northern Ireland elections, and that it was not unknown for the dead to 'vote', propagandists would naturally

7.2

7.3

IN
REMEMBRANCE OF

MR JOSEPH DEVLIN, M.P.
THE PEOPLES' FRIEND.

assert that it was a practice of their opponents – and of them alone.

In any case, with or without the help of the dead, Devlin held his Westminster seat from 1902 until he died in 1934 (no. 7.3). In addition, he was the only non-Unionist to win a seat for a Belfast constituency in the Northern Ireland parliamentary elections of May 1921. He then led the Nationalist Party of Northern Ireland but did not enter the local assembly until 1925. As the leading constitutional nationalist of his era, in Northern Ireland, Devlin was an obvious target for unionist wit.

Republicans, of course refused to play any part in Northern Ireland politics. Devlin was rightly recognised by unionists as their most effective opponent, and conversely, the death of the 'People's Friend' in January 1934 robbed nationalists of whatever limited political leadership they had experienced since 1920. The issue of memorial cards, of which No. 7.3, is but one typical example, would not therefore be unexpected.

Lamenting his loss, the *Irish News* of 19th January wrote the following in the course of a lengthy eulogy:

> Because of the sorrow that is universal, one leaves aside for the moment, the glories that were his; the abiding achievements that crowned his historic triumphs; even the struggles that brought him close to the heart of the people. His fame will not grow dim in the years that are to come. Though values set on men's worth shift and change, his memory will endure.

With that level of adulation, a postcard (no. 7.3), based on one of his more recent photographs, appears almost as an anti-climax. There is evidence, though certainly not in postcard form, that Devlin was well respected even by his Unionist opponents.

Some pictorial record of Northern Ireland's experience during the Second World War could reasonably have been expected. Photographs of bomb damage in Belfast, as a result of German air-raids, are well-known, though security reasons would probably have limited their publication at the time. While some photographs of this type may exist in postcard form, no trace of them could be found. Only

7.4

"TOBY" 512 Oldpark Road, Belfast.
For Belfast Telegraph "Spitfire" Fund.

an oblique reference to the War was discovered (no. 7.4).

This featured Toby, a performing dog used by his owner Sam Corry of Oldpark Road Belfast, to raise funds for the war effort. Through his tricks, such as riding a scooter, and sounding a horn, the partnership raised in excess of £200 for the *Belfast Telegraph*'s 'Spitfire Fund'. Another contemporary picture, also produced in postcard form, described this clever canine as being 'On Active Service'.

No post-war political issue in Northern Ireland appears to have spawned a political postcard. Nothing else could be traced until 1966, when once again political developments were reflected in postcard form.

In this case, (no. 7.5), the Northern Ireland cartoonist Rowel Friers has taken an essentially non-political and humorous look at Irish politics. Nelson's Pillar, or simply 'The Pillar,' as it was more commonly called, was probably the best known and familiar landmark in Dublin, since it was erected in 1808. From time-to-time Irish nationalists had argued with varying degrees of intensity, that it should be replaced, as it represented for them an obvious and unwelcome link with the former British presence in Ireland.

In March 1966, most likely to 'commemorate' the 50th anniversary of the Easter Rising, the IRA planted explosives, which demolished about three quarters of the monument. Subsequently, the Irish Army had to

7.5

"IT'S A LITTLE SOUVENIR I BOUGHT FROM DUBLIN DEAR."

COURTESY YVONNE FRIERS

7.6

complete the job in the interests of safety. The remnants of the Pillar, like those of the Berlin Wall, almost a quarter of a century later, became much sought after as souvenirs. In our example, our gallant gentleman has brought the wife more than the usual stick of rock. This was the setting for Frier's gentle humour, which makes a refreshing change from the frequently grim history of Northern Ireland.

Another page of that sad history was turned in August 1969. Then Derry street violence, following the Apprentice Boys march, escalated and overflowed into Belfast, where traditional sectarian violence, once again flared, necessitating the deployment of British troops on the streets of both cities.

7.7

7.8

Although the Army was initially welcomed by nationalists, relations with the troops had soured within a year. Then an upsurge of violence inspired a rush of political propaganda, some of it in the form of postcards.

Despite continuing destruction of property and a rising death toll, it was impossible to suppress the Belfast sense of humour, as the captions on the reverse of these pictures of rioters reveal (nos. 7.6, 7.7 and 7.8). This is not to deny for a moment that bitterness ran deeper and wider, as one tragic event followed another. Regarding 'Returning the empties', there was a real advertising campaign in Northern Ireland to encourage just that. It was considered necessary as so many bottles were put to other uses during rioting in the early years of the 'Troubles'. Far-fetched though it seems, it may even have contributed in some small way to the demise of the milk bottle and its replacement by the carton! A much harder edge to the caption, in this much more recent production from Derry in 1990 (no. 7.9), shows but a glimmer of the growing rancour, in its parody of a current Army recruiting campaign (Join the Army. See The World). It might just be noted in passing that Novick in his study of nationalist propaganda during the First World War, commented on how Irish nationalists transformed recruiting material into counter-propaganda. On the reverse of this card, distributed by the 'Bloody Sunday Initiative', the following was printed,

Join the British Army
See the world, visit exotic places,
Meet interesting people …
And kill them.

7.9

The use of these and similar postcards for general propaganda purposes is very evident. Much of it was focused on foreign opinion in particular. This picture of a 'Provo Patrol' (no. 7.10), one of a series produced by 'the Republican Movement,' was guaranteed to inflame local unionist opinion, but much more importantly, it was meant to appeal to the rosy romantic notion of some Irish-Americans, ready to contribute their dollars to the 'cause.' The message is simplistic and really requires no understanding of the Northern Ireland problem.

Revolutionary greetings from Ireland

7.10

7.11

Many other cards are similar in style to this. In general, they attack British policies, such as internment, strip-searching of prisoners, or the use of rubber bullets, which feature on several cards. In this specific instance, (no. 7.11), the image of the doll and the chalked body outline is both very simple and effective. Many of the cards do not refer to specific incidents. Bloody Sunday (one Linen Hall Library example), 'the Birmingham 6' (three Linen Hall examples), and above all else the republican hunger strike(s) might be viewed as obvious exceptions. The last of these

7.12

7.13

BOBY SANDS   (5 MAI)
FRANCIS HUGHES   (12 MAI)
RAY MC CREESH   (21 MAI)
PATSY O'HARA   (22 MAI)
JOE MC DONNELL   (8 JUILLET)
MARTIN HURSON   (13 JUILLET)
KEVIN LYNCH   (1 AOUT)
KIERAN DOHERTY   (2 AOUT)
THOMAS MC ELWEE   (8 AOUT)
MICHAEL DEVINE   (20 AOUT)

29 Juillet 1981   MARIAGE DU SIECLE...
le Prince Charles enterre sa vie de garçon"...
... les Irlandais enterrent leurs grévistes de la faim !!!
MAGGIE, ARRETEZ LE MASSACRE, S.V.P. !!!

was a tragedy, but was also, arguably the republican's greatest propaganda success, which was exploited both at home and abroad, and its importance was certainly reflected in the number of cards which it spawned.

The withdrawal of 'special category' status from Republican prisoners sowed the seeds for the hunger strikes of 1980 and 1981. The dispute which ensued, escalated from the refusal of prisoners to wear prison clothes, to the 'Dirty Protest', and then in October 1980 to the first hunger strike. These earlier stages of the protest drew interest from abroad, and were recorded in postcard form, as in this Dutch example (no. 7.12 LIN). The political message on the placards is self-explanatory.

International interest in the second major hunger strike was indicated in this example from the 'Modern Events' series issued in France (no. 7.13). It draws a rather grisly comparison between the 'Just Married' Charles and Diana, and the 'Just Dead' hunger-strikers. It will be observed that it is laid out in the form of a memorial card giving the name and date of death for each of the hunger-strikers.

The French caption begs 'Maggie' (Thatcher) to end this slaughter, and reinforces the pictorial message by stating that Charles has just buried his boyhood, after 'the marriage of the century,' as the Irish have buried their named hunger-strikers. Although this postcard would be of very limited help in analysing this episode of our history, it does, nevertheless, confirm the international impact of their deaths.

A picture of Bobby Sands carried in procession through the Paris streets would tend to reinforce that conclusion (no. 7.14). One would, of course have to qualify that conclusion in the absence of knowledge about the size of the crowd and the duration of the impact. Does it represent a widespread feeling or merely an extremist fringe? Similarly, the influence of the previous card would probably be restricted by the fact that it was one of a limited edition of 1,500 only.

Propaganda, originally designed for home consumption, in the form of a mural, is well-represented in this further example (no. 7.15). The naked corpse, draped in

7.14

an Irish tricolour loincloth, is borne by a man, probably the victim's father, closely supported by his mother. All this is set against the back-drop of a prison camp, whose watch-towers dominate the skyline. Lest there be the slightest doubt about the intended message, the scene is titled 'Long Kesh 1981', and the top left-hand corner displays a poster with the appeal, 'Support the H Block Strikers'.

The central figure undoubtedly represents Bobby Sands, IRA leader in Long Kesh (a.k.a. The Maze Prison), MP for Fermanagh-South Tyrone, and the first of the hunger-strikers to die. In some respects, the picture is reminiscent of the *Pieta*, and this is undoubtedly the sort of image the artist would attempt to evoke, although many others would find that both deeply offensive and blasphemous.

7.15

It is highly likely that the analogy of the naked body, representing Christ taken down from the Cross, with the republican 'blanket protest', the refusal of IRA prisoners to wear prison clothes, is also intended. While the mural itself was originally for home consumption, as it were, the issue of the postcard could widen its appeal both nationally and internationally.

The identification of the republican dead with the Crucifixion, the ultimate martyrdom, should be seen as a continuation of a tradition rooted in the immediate aftermath of the Easter Rising. There were several explicit comparisons in post-Rising written propaganda. Novick discusses Pearse's 'self-created similarity to Christ', while others went so far as to equate Ireland to Christ. The symbolism of the whole Easter period is so obvious that it verges on becoming a cliché.

Consciously, unconsciously or even subconsciously, and one leans heavily towards the first option, the artist has drawn on traditional nationalist imagery. Although the linkage to the executed of 1916 is the most obvious, this depiction of an Irish nationalist predates the 1916 Rising. Sean Moran, in a collection of essays, entitled *Images, Icons and the Irish Nationalist Imagination* pointed out that nationalist cartoons during the Land War of the 1880s, 'tended to turn political and agrarian leaders into saints and martyrs,' while L.W. McBride, editor of the same work drew attention to a cartoon of 1893 in the *Irish Weekly Independent*, showing a *Pieta*-like image of Parnell supported by a militant Erin, and there is at least one similar depiction of the Manchester Martyrs of 1867. Unquestionably, and irrespective of the views of critics, it is clear from this card, from other murals, some reproduced as cards, and from his quotations on other republican cards, that Sands has been added to the top tier of the republican pantheon.

7.16

While Bobby Sands was the first hunger-striker to die, Michael Devine, shown in this charcoal sketch (no. 7.16) was the last. Unlike the majority of these victims, he was not a member of the IRA, but rather of the much smaller INLA, two of whose members died on strike. Each of the ten strikers who died was featured on a similar card in the same series.

The content of these most recent cards falls a long way short of

7.17

adequately conveying the appalling suffering of the last twenty-five years and more. Indeed it is exceedingly doubtful if either the printed word or painted picture could do that successfully. A partisan approach, which is a feature of nearly all these cards (more or less), ensured that no-one tried to portray the overall picture.

Nothing better illustrates the partisan nature of the cards and the depths of division in Northern Ireland than attitudes to the security forces, with special republican antipathy reserved for those which were local in nature. There are, at the very least, several cards in the Linen Hall Library collection from a range of sources attacking the RUC. They are shown saturating republican areas during Republican funerals, presumably to prevent paramilitary displays, are condemned for 'murder' by rubber bullets, and some include the demand to the government 'Disband the RUC.'

Some examples focus on the UDR and collusion with loyalist paramilitaries. Sometimes the allegations are generalised and sweeping, but in this case, (no. 7.17 LIN), reference is to a very specific incident, on 31st July 1975, when three members of the popular Miami Showband were gunned down outside Banbridge, with two UVF members, who were also serving members of the UDR, dying from their own bomb during the attack, and other UDR men subsequently being given 35 year jail sentences for their part in the affair. It was initially puzzling that the artist appeared to have given the UDR man an RUC cap, a most unlikely error. It is of course a none-too-subtle attempt to implicate them also in the killings. In the concluding lines of an article in the *Sunday Business Post* on the thirtieth anniversary of the atrocity, the journalist Tom Mc Gurk summed up thus, 'Whether these activities were unilateral or a wider part of British intelligence undercover activity remains the most significant question.' This is but one of several questions unanswered about this particular atrocity and indeed of many others, which it is not the function of this work to answer.

The dichotomy of attitudes to the security forces could hardly be more clearly displayed, when the above is compared with the loyalist mural/postcard and its

7.18

message, "WHO WILL DEFEND ULSTER NOW? (7.18). That can of course also be read as a self-justification on the part of loyalist paramilitaries for their own existence. As long as such a chasm existed in republican and loyalist attitudes towards the forces of law and order in Northern Ireland, it was difficult to be optimistic about political progress. The development and wider acceptance of the PSNI has offered greater hope.

Loyalist cards just as much as those from a nationalist viewpoint also fail to reflect the overall tragedy of the situation. Partisanship is equally shared but there is a slight difference in treatment. More than is the case for republican material, their examples are much more generalised. Indeed it is only very rarely indeed that they deal with specific events of the 'Troubles', as in this reproduction of a mural commemorating one of the more prominent victims of the IRA (no. 7.19).

The Reverend Robert Bradford worked as a Methodist minister in the Lenadoon/Suffolk area of West

7.19

7.20

Belfast. In 1973, he had stood as a Vanguard candidate for the constituency of South Antrim. Founded by William Craig, the erstwhile hardline Northern Ireland Minister of Home Affairs, this organisation represented unionists who were alarmed by the apparently reformist and compromising tendencies of Brian Faulkner's government.

Although his first foray into politics proved unsuccessful, Robert Bradford had only a short wait before making his breakthrough. In 1974, he was elected to serve at Westminster as member for South Belfast. Seven years later, at a community centre in Finaghy, he was shot dead by a Provisional IRA gang of five on 14th November 1981.

Some commentators have speculated that this murder was an attempt by Republicans to stir up a massive loyalist backlash. In 1981, the year of the hunger strike, tensions were already running very high in nationalist circles, and loyalist retaliation on a large scale might have made Northern Ireland just about ungovernable. No-one knows the sort of contingency plans the government might have implemented under those circumstances. There is a certain logic in this hypothesis, but there is absolutely no hard evidence to substantiate it, unless it exists in security files not yet available to the public, and unlikely to be so for many years to come.

Although violent events on the streets of Northern Ireland stimulated the production of other loyalist cards, they largely ignored the current political scene, even to a more marked extent than republican material. Almost without exception, they looked to the past, as in the Derry wall mural (no. 7.20) or the batch of cards reproduced from the era of the 1912 Home Rule crisis (eg. nos. 7.21 to 7.23).

7.21

7.22

7.23

The first of these, which has been regularly reproduced in books, stresses the continuity of our 'Troubles'. It clearly commemorates the 'Relief of Derry, 1689.' It was originally painted in the Fountain Estate, a small Protestant enclave on the Catholic west bank (or "cityside" of Derry), during the 1920s, when the city and much of Ireland was in turbulence and the Protestant minority here obviously felt under siege once again. Its reproduction in the most recent troubles and of the others is really another case of history being seen to repeat itself.

A comprehensive, if maybe not exhaustive study of other loyalist cards, 40 in total, depicting loyalist graffiti/wall art is quite revealing.

CONTENT	TOTAL
Crests with/without slogan	22
Appeal for Loyalist Prisoners	7
Memorials to Paramilitaries	6
1912 Home Rule Crisis	3
General Fighting Prowess	3
1690/Boyne	2
Somme 1916	2
Specific reference to 1969–	1

It may be noted that the numbers quoted slightly exceed the number of cards. The apparent discrepancy is explained by the fact that a few cards contain material thought relevant in more than a single category. Some of this is self-explanatory but a little further analysis is apt.

Paramilitary crests are as one would expect of the UVF, UDA, UYM, UFF, RHC, YCV and PAF. Sometimes two or three appear on the same mural. A range of slogans includes 'Simply the Best', 'Compromise or Conflict', 'Resist Éire Involvement' and 'Ulster's Destiny Is In Our Hands. Our Grip Is Tight. We'll Never Let Go.'

One of the references to loyalist fighting prowess shows what one takes to be Johnny 'Mad Dog' Adair, once beloved but no longer, of the UDA, with Union Jack singlet and bulldog like features, driving a Jerry Adams-look-a-like cur in Celtic jersey out of the Shankill in the imagined direction of Dublin. The only specific reference to 'military activities' post-1969 is some very black humour referring to an attack by rocket launcher on Sinn Féin premises in 1994.

In every case the traditional loyalist message was simple, direct and negative. The Williamite mural said 'No' to the army of James II. Nos 18 to 20 here said 'No' to Home Rule, and the most recent wall-painting repeated a similar slogan on the map of Northern Ireland (no. 7.24).

The fact that loyalist work rarely referred to specific events may suggest that its purpose was less propagandist, more to raise funds for those loyalist groups, such

7.24

as the UDA and Ulster Clubs who published much of it. In any case, their common and central message is a simple rejection of change. Perhaps that attitude which has, or at least had until fairly recently, prevailed on all sides for a very long time is an accurate reflection of the nature of our troubles.

8

SOUTHERN IRELAND
1923–ONWARDS

Introduction

Southern Ireland existed in law, (if not in practice), from 1920 until 1921 only, but it is a convenient term to describe the Irish political unit excluding Northern Ireland, which was variously known at different times as the Irish Free State, Éire or the Republic of Ireland.

Southern politics after 1923 were dominated by recovery from Civil War, state-building and the reintegration of most anti-Treatyites into the structures of the state soon after the formation of Fianna Fáil. The 1930s were marked by De Valera's efforts to revise the Treaty and the 'Economic War' with Britain. The most notable feature of the War period 1939–45 or what they called the 'Emergency' was Irish neutrality. The late 1950s and 60s were marked by economic development, and a less isolationist attitude towards the rest of the world, although the Southern Irish attitude to Partition remained as an ever-present backdrop throughout the whole period.

It was only the latter issue, which was reflected to any noticeable extent in postcards, with a trickle throughout the period, and a blip in 1966 particularly with the garish commemorative productions of Irish Art Publications. The major explanation for this dearth of material was simply that the Golden Age of postcards was already past by the early 1920s, for reasons which are mentioned elsewhere. A certain war-weariness by 1923 after the tumultuous 1916–23 period could also have been a contributory factor. Nevertheless, at least one local political issue and several national ones fleetingly engaged the attention of postcard producers.

* * * * *

The Irish Free State of the mid-twenties suffered from the aftershocks of the violent decade which had preceded it, in particular, the Civil War. Nowhere was this highlighted more clearly than in the assassination of Kevin O'Higgins on 10th July 1927 (no. 8.1).

O'Higgins was a hate figure for anti-Treaty republicans. His position alone, as Minister of Justice and Home Affairs, was probably sufficient to make him a target, but the policies he supported during and after the Civil War were of greater significance.

The late KEVIN O'HIGGINS, Minister for Justice, Irish Free State.
Photo Lafayette. Dublin.

8.1

O'Higgins was blamed for the Army Powers Act in the autumn of 1922, although its passing resulted from a collective government decision. This legislation established Military Courts with power to impose the death penalty. Seventy-seven republicans had been shot as a result. Undoubtedly the most ruthless act was the cold-blooded execution in December 1922 of four leading republican prisoners, namely Barrett, Mc Kelvey, Mellows and O'Connor. This was done as a very deliberate high-profile reprisal for the murder of a TD the previous day. The subsequent government statement was chilling. It said that the killing of the four was: '… a solemn warning to those associated with them who are engaged in the conspiracy of assassination against the Representatives of the Irish people.'(Macardle pg. 823). The policy was an effective deterrent for the time being but republicans have very long memories.

After the Civil War, O'Higgins had prime responsibility for Public Safety Acts in 1923, 1924 and 1926. In essence, they legalised internment of IRA men. Ironically the murder of O'Higgins proved beneficial for democracy, since Cosgrave's government reacted to it by passing the Electoral Amendment Act of 1927, requiring candidates for the Dáil to take the Oath of Allegiance enshrined in the 1922 Treaty. Paradoxically this provided an excuse for De Valera to end his abstentionist policy by bringing his followers into the Dáil (see Hickey and Doherty, pp 123–4, for further details).

A further echo of the earlier 'Troubles' can be seen in the 1929 commemoration at Dublin's Deansgrange Cemetery (no. 8.2). Reginald Dunne and Joseph O'Sullivan were executed at Wandsworth Prison in London for the murder of Sir Henry Wilson in June 1922. Wilson could be seen as a unionist mirror-image of Kevin O'Higgins. He had been an outspoken critic of British government policy in Ireland during the Anglo-Irish War. Wilson had argued that the Army needed

DUNNE AND O'SULLIVAN MEMORIAL 11TH AUGUST '29 . DEANSGRANGE   8.2

to be given a much freer hand, and had gone so far as to suggest that the best way to end the violence would be to shoot Sinn Féin leaders in an open and official policy of reprisal. In 1922, he was special security advisor to James Craig, Prime Minister of Northern Ireland, and some Irish nationalists had blamed him for sectarian attacks against Catholics during the Northern Troubles.

In an interesting flashback to cards previously quoted (nos. 3.16 and 5.16), and a host of others on a similar theme, Keith Jeffery in his *Ireland and the Great War* (p.65) quotes from a statement drawn up for their trial by Dunne on behalf of himself and O'Sullivan, explaining how they, both former British soldiers, became responsible for the murder of the ex-Head of the Imperial General Staff:

> We both joined voluntarily for the purpose of taking human life, in order that the principles for which this country stood should be upheld and preserved. These principles, we were told, were Self-Determination and Freedom for Small Nations … We came back from France to find that Self-Determination had been given to some Nations we had never heard of, but that it had been denied to Ireland.

Although there was certainly a revival of IRA activity towards the end of the 1920s, the commemoration shown in this card may be nothing more than a memorial service for Dunne and O'Sullivan close to the anniversary of their execution (10th August). On the other hand, republicans have never been in the least inclined to hide their light under a bushel. It can be viewed as a mark of respect to former colleagues, a record for their followers, and an invitation to prospective recruits.

The question of partition remained constantly as an issue, and it was again featured in a postcard of the late 1940s or early 1950s (it is believed).

beannact na peile pádraig

When thinking of Ireland
on St. Patrick's Day
remember—

Slemish

Armagh
Downpatrick

* That the Irish nation has been
partitioned by Britain against the
will of the overwhelming majority
of the people ;

* That the essence of democratic
rule is contained in the right of a
people to determine its own affairs
without outside interference ;

* That St. Patrick's See at Armagh,
his grave at Downpatrick and the
scenes of his boyhood on Slemish
are cut off from the body of Ireland
and are in the area occupied by
British troops in a flagrant denial
of all democratic rights.

On this St. Patrick's Day
pledge yourself to help to
undo the dismemberment
of St. Patrick's Island

B. & N., LTD.   DUBLIN.

8.3

A Saint Patrick's Day card (no. 8.3), with its greeting in Irish, has been used to argue for the reunification of Ireland on historical, democratic, religious and geographical grounds. One would have to think that the target audience for this message was primarily Irish-American. The text on the card is self-explanatory. It may be associated with The Anti-Partition League.

'Free The Murrays Now!' (no. 8.4) also originated from political violence but its subjects were Irish anarchists rather than nationalists. Noel and Marie Murray were supporters of the Anarchist Black Cross, on whose behalf they had previously raised funds by conventional and legal means. This organisation had been established about 1920 during Civil War in Russia as part of 'an international class struggle and anarchist prisoner support group'. It folded in the 1940s only to be revived in 1960s Britain, mainly in support of Anti-Franco prisoners in Spain.

By 1975 the Murrays had resorted to less conventional fundraising, namely armed bank robbery. During a raid on a Dublin bank Marie Murray fired a shot which killed Garda Michael Reynolds. A claim by supporters that she was not wearing her glasses and consequently 'accidentally shot a policeman in plain clothes' did not convince the court, and she was convicted of capital murder. However, her sentence was commuted to life imprisonment, the same sentence as was passed on her husband. Some of their supporters waged a publicity campaign against the sentences. This included a visit by the philosopher and writer Jean Paul Sartre to Dublin, a brief occupation of Aer Lingus offices in London and this postcard. The ineffectiveness of this campaign might be gauged from the fact that the Murrays served eighteen years in prison.

During the first decade of the Free State's existence, only two occurrences were deemed of sufficient importance to spawn a series of postcards. One was economic, the other religious. Neither was political in the narrowest sense of the word and yet each had political ramifications

8.4

Postcards in general are poor at examining economic issues, which do not readily lend themselves to pictorial presentation. Thus for example, the greatest economic issues from the end of the 1920s onward were unemployment, and the economic fallout from De Valera's determination to revise the Treaty and in particular his refusal to pay Land Annuities to Britain. Contemporary Irish postcards did not reflect any of that. In fact, the only economic development to be depicted in a range of postcards was the Shannon hydro-electric scheme.

This project, in and around Ardnacrusha, near Limerick, was the first major state investment undertaken by the Free State government. The construction period lasted from 1925 until 1929 (no. 8.5). An Electricity Supply Act was passed in

8.5

1927, creating the ESB, which was given the task of generating power and administering a national grid.

Not everyone benefited equally from this scheme in its earliest years, because the first power generated was for industrial and urban use alone. Rural electrification was not completed until after the Second World War. Nevertheless, this scheme was the first important step in a process, which arguably brought greater benefit to a larger number of people, than all the political posturing and constitutional conjuring tricks of the previous decades.

The major religious phenomenon was the Dublin Eucharistic Congress of 1932. Towards the end of June that year, it brought together many thousands of Catholics from all corners of Ireland and abroad. It was of course primarily a religious and not a political event, and yet it had political significance. One historian considered that it, '... marked a great fusion of Catholic and nationalist pride and probably made a contribution to healing Civil War wounds.' (S.J. Connolly). It was the first opportunity since independence for Catholic Ireland to preen itself before the world.

The Congress occurred at an especially delicate stage in Anglo-Irish relations. At a time when De Valera, the Republican bogeyman, had just assumed power, and when he was in the midst of a well-publicised dispute with the British government over his attempt to abolish both the Oath of Allegiance and the payment of Land Annuities, a great display of Catholic fervour was enough to touch a raw nerve in the north. In celebration of the Congress, Catholic areas of Northern Ireland were bedecked with Congress and Papal Flags, bunting and arches. Catholic Ireland was on the march and it proved just too much for some. On several occasions, Catholic pilgrims going to the Congress were attacked. If we examine contemporary newspaper reports, we can see that the *Irish Times* for example, played the matter down in comparison to the *Irish News*. It still reported on the 29th June that the Limerick Diocesan Synod of the Church of Ireland declared 'our indignation at the

8.6

cowardly attacks made by some so-called Protestants …', and in similar fashion the Coleraine Protestant Ministers' Council condemned 'an unwarranted attack' on Catholics en route to Dublin. Over the border in Buncrana, notices appeared, calling for a retaliatory boycott of Protestant firms, although no evidence was found that it materialised.

This postcard, only one of many produced for the Congress, is no more than one of many inoffensive souvenirs of a major religious festival (no. 8.6). The Irish motto means 'God Save Ireland'. If unionist extremists had been aware that it could also be translated as 'God Free Ireland', it might have caused more controversy and even violence. It is, however, most unlikely that this or any other politicisation of the Congress was intended.

At the same time, it needs to be recognised that the slogan on this card and the song 'God Save Ireland' have strongly political origins, being associated with the executed Fenians, Allen, Larkin and O'Brien, remembered as the Manchester Martyrs. The use of the motto here could be construed as an argument for the enduring, pervasive and subliminal influence of Irish nationalist propaganda. It is discomfiting to realise that it is probably more deeply-rooted in the nationalist psyche than many would care to admit.

Two further cards only were traced from the period after 1932 until the early 1960s. The first of these had a peripheral relevance to Ireland and would not be worthy of even passing notice except that it is representative of a particular and popular *genre* of postcards. This is a flimsy example of Bamforth 'Comic' cards, making reference in name to the state established by the Treaty and which retained the same name until the 1937 Constitution, and drawing on the tradition of feeble *double entendre*, of seaside landladies, busty blondes and toilet humour. Some may think it appropriate that it was posted from Blackpool (no. 8.7)!

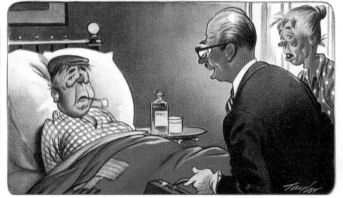

8.7

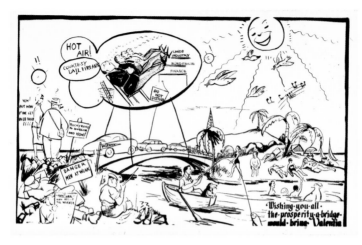

8.8

The second offers some more subtle humour and holds greater interest. In this case, a single card highlights a local political issue (no. 8.8). Valentia Island, off the Kerry coast, holds its own little niche in the history of telecommunications, as the European end of the trans-Atlantic cable from 1866 until 1965, when satellite technology rendered cables obsolete. Ironically, after the closure in 1960 of its railway link, which had run from 1893, the island was isolated. That is the context for this humorous card. To the right we have the vision of 'Paradise Island', Valentia-style, of sun and sand complete with its Royal [sic] Yacht club, while visitors travel in over the newly constructed bridge.

On the other side we have harsh reality. Prospective tourists, no doubt wealthy Americans – he with his fat cigar – are stranded landside on 'the rocky road to Dublin.' The 'DANGER MEN AT WORK' sign, presumably referring to those supposedly constructing the bridge, is belied by the activities of those reclining on

Spellbound 8.9

Committee For The Rights Of Travellers
01, Virginia Heights, Tallaght, Co. Dublin

Published by
Women's Community Press
48 Fleet Street, Dublin 2. Tel: 712149

8.10

ENNIS/O'GORMAN

Political and church leaders have been responsible for increasing negative attitudes to Travellers. Politicians of all shades of opinions have publicly vented anti-traveller attitudes to further their own political ends. The Church has failed to denounce the cruel evictions of Travellers by Local Authoritites and

54

the shore. Meanwhile, far away in Dublin at the Dáil, hot air abounds, while Ministers loll undisturbed by the island's plight.

For once the news is good – a tribute perhaps to postcard power. A bridge was eventually constructed in 1970 across the channel at Portmagee. Its impact may not have been quite as depicted by the artist.

The remaining, more recent, cards are also about protest, two dealing with public policy on major social issues, another almost impossible to classify, and the rest concentrating on concerns of a wider national and international nature.

The two social issues which surfaced in postcards referred to women and Travellers (nos. 8.9 and 8.10). Both make a simple, effective point using an identical artistic device, namely a signpost. Both are believed, one with near certainty, the other more tentatively, to belong to the 1980s, and somewhat ironically, while both refer specifically to the Republic of Ireland, they have been preserved not in the Republic but in Belfast's Linen Hall Library.

No. 8.9 uses the signpost '*Fir*' (most frequently seen pointing to the nearest 'Gents') in combination with 'The Four Courts' to indicate where the male-dominated judiciary adjudicate on the law, in such a way that women (*Mná*)) have only one way to go, namely on 'The Ferry To Britain.' Most people in the Republic would understand the point being made without further elaboration, but just in case, there should be the slightest doubt, the reverse of the card gives locations and phone numbers of several Pregnancy Counselling Services. The broad context of this is the Republic's ban on abortion, which the pro-life lobby copper-fastened in 1983 with a legal amendment. Irrespective of this, and further amendments, many

Irish women have continued to go annually to Britain for abortions. (UK. Dept. of Health statistics). The issue remains highly relevant to the present day. Indeed postcards have again been used in the ongoing campaign about proposals to amend the law, so that it would permit abortion in limited circumstances.

According to Pavee Point, an organisation which represents their interests, there are about 30,000 Travellers, a disadvantaged ethnic minority, resident in the Republic of Ireland.

Since a Dáil report in 1983, it has been official policy that Travellers should not only have government recognition, but that they should be given accommodation. Some local authorities have taken this much more seriously than others, but the overall results have been poor until recently. Statistics quoted in the *Encyclopaedia of Ireland* show that by the year 2000 only 1,152 families had been housed on legal sites with basic facilities, a further 380 on housing schemes specifically for Travellers, and 2,110 in local authority housing. Local authorities have had a statutory duty to house Travellers since 2000, but have fallen well-short of requirements. As recently as 1998, it was calculated that as many as 24 per cent of Travellers lived in unserviced sites or by the side of the road. The writer of this article summed up thus: 'Since the 1960s local authorities have actively penalised the nomadic life-style, not least through the systematic blocking of traditional campsites and a refusal to implement state guidelines on accommodation' (see *The Encyclopedia of Ireland*, 2003).

This is the general context in which card no. 8.10 was issued. The signpost clearly highlights the unpleasant options they have been offered. The cry of helplessness spells out their plight and the caption on the back indicts both church and state for either their prejudice or lack of positive action. The two leading political figures of the 1980s, Charles Haughey and Garret Fitzgerald, can be easily identified and similarly in another card not featured here.

A newspaper article in the *Sunday Independent* of 13th April 2013 paints a more optimistic picture. It quotes an Irish government report to an EU justice and equality body that €370 million has been spent between 2000 and 2010 on provision of housing and other halting site accommodation for Travellers.

It may seem a shade surprising that the Northern Ireland crisis from 1968 onwards appears to have scarcely impinged on postcard production in the Republic of Ireland. One might validly pose the question, 'Should anything be read into that?'

With the exception of the labelled Republican Movement cards mentioned elsewhere, which, barring one or two, bear no publisher's address, but which deal with Northern Ireland specifically, although possibly emanating from the South, only two cards have been traced. One of these deals with the marginal matter of Margaretta D'Arcy's play.

Margaretta D'Arcy has led a life of protest for the last half-century. She is an Anglo-Irish, Russo-Jewish, ex-Sinn Féin socialist dramatist with anarchist and strong pacifist leanings! Having taken up residence in Ireland in 1968, she became involved in the civil rights movement in Galway. Her play, written in 1972, in collaboration with the Barnsley dramatist John Arden (her husband) attacked inequality, the British Army and the IRA. A production of this play was brought to an early close after objections from senior military figures and a libel action against the author.

The blurb on this postcard (no. 8.11), published by Countercards of Pontefract, protests about censorship of her play, *About Ireland and British oppression*. Like Margaretta D'Arcy herself, the card is difficult to categorise, but it has enough of Ireland and politics in it to justify its inclusion in this selection.

Slightly more central is an appeal to Taoiseach, John Bruton (1994–7)

8.11

from the Irish National Congress under the heading 'Peace Cannot Be Built On Partition' (not illustrated), which asks that there be no dilution of Articles 2 and 3 of the Irish Constitution, which laid claim to Northern Ireland. For a considerable time before the signing of the Belfast Agreement of 1998 it was known that discussion of these clauses was taking place, and the Republic's claim was eventually replaced in the redrafting by an aspiration.

8.12

135

8.13

Two further cards, while retaining an Irish focus, introduce an international angle in objecting to President Reagan's visit to Ireland in June 1984 (nos. 8.12 and 8.13). Both were produced by the Women's Community Press, the first of them for the Student Christian Movement. In number 8.12 hostility to Reagan stems from the threat of nuclear war on 'nuclear free' Ireland. no. 8.13, on first impression, would appear to be no more than a lame joke about the 'Special Relationship' between Britain and the USA, especially the rapport between Maggie Thatcher and Ronald Reagan. However, the caption on the reverse enlightens us with a far sharper message: 'NO WELCOME FOR RAYGUN – SYMBOL OF CAPITALISM, WARMONGERING AND U.S. IMPERIALISM'. Somehow it has a familiar ring in the context of the 2004 Bush visit to Ireland.

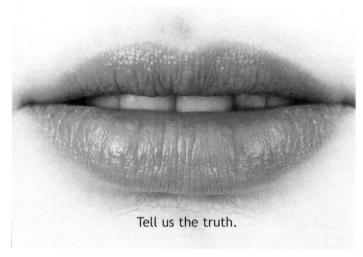

Tell us the truth.

8.14

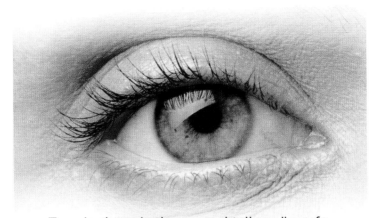

Tony, Look me in the eye and tell me I'm safe.   8.15

Opposition to Reagan's visit to Ireland was more widespread than the radical student fringe. Even the Catholic hierarchy, in particular Bishop Casey of Galway, who had worked on the missions in Central America, was unhappy with Reagan's Central American policies, which included involvement in Nicaragua, the invasion of the Caribbean island of Grenada in October 1983, and above all, his support for the right-wing junta in El Salvador. During the Irish visit, a group of Irish priests and nuns led a mock funeral procession, in protest at the murders of religious in El Salvador.

There was also widespread concern and criticism of Reagan's support for the development of nuclear missile systems. (Hence the 'Raygun' pun.) Put simply, Reagan's visit to Ireland was not quite the unadulterated propaganda coup he might have hoped for in his quest for re-election. In any case, his victory in the presidential election race was sufficiently decisive to render any few votes he may have gained through his Irish visit of little consequence, and certainly the opposition to his policies shown in these cards proved singularly ineffective.

Fear of nuclear power, specifically the threat to Ireland from the nuclear reprocessing plant at Sellafield in Cumbria, lies behind three more recent cards of rather subtler humour, which were issued in recent years on behalf of the Chernobyl Children's Project (nos 8.14, 8.15 and 8.16). This charity was established in 1990, by Adi Roche, just less than five years after the nuclear disaster at Chernobyl in the Ukraine. It has been described by the United Nations as 'the worst environmental catastrophe in the history of humanity'. An estimated three to four million children were affected. The food supply has been contaminated, and even the gene pool has been affected, so that children not yet born will almost certainly continue to suffer the consequences. Amongst other activities, this charity sends convoys of medical supplies and other aid to the region, and it has brought thousands of children out of Belarus, Ukraine and Russia for rest and recuperation.

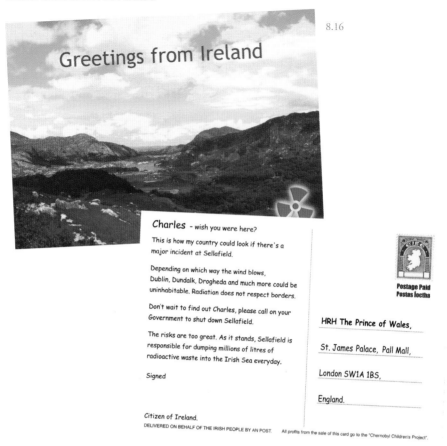

8.16

Greetings from Ireland

Charles - wish you were here?

This is how my country could look if there's a major incident at Sellafield.

Depending on which way the wind blows, Dublin, Dundalk, Drogheda and much more could be uninhabitable. Radiation does not respect borders.

Don't wait to find out Charles, please call on your Government to shut down Sellafield.

The risks are too great. As it stands, Sellafield is responsible for dumping millions of litres of radioactive waste into the Irish Sea everyday.

Signed

Citizen of Ireland.

DELIVERED ON BEHALF OF THE IRISH PEOPLE BY AN POST.   All profits from the sale of this card go to the "Chernobyl Children's Project".

Postage Paid
Postas Íoctha

HRH The Prince of Wales,

St. James Palace, Pall Mall,

London SW1A 1BS,

England.

The cards were addressed on behalf of the Irish people to Norman Askew, chief executive of British Nuclear Fuels, to Tony Blair and to HRH The Prince of Wales. Each had a pre-printed address on the reverse. All are similar, but each is tailored to the image on the card and to the recipient. Tony Blair's message on the reverse of number 8.15 contains the phrase, 'Don't be blind to the danger, Tony'.

All three cards are cleverly designed, but the 'Greetings from Ireland' (no. 8.16) example stands out. The unnatural colouring of sky and land is immediately eye-catching, and the metamorphosis of the shamrock into the radiation warning symbol is particularly striking.

Prince Charles was an astute choice of recipient for no. 8.16, because of his known concern for the environment (see illustration on reverse side). To send many thousands of these cards was a clever marketing ploy. Their effectiveness, however, is another question. In their favour, it might be argued that they illustrated to the Irish government, even though it was not the target audience, how strongly many people felt and it may have contributed to their taking international, legal action against the British government over the issue.

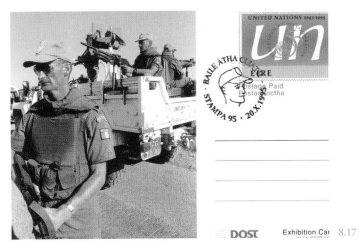

DOST   Exhibition Car   8.17

This final specimen (no. 8.17) more clearly reflects Irish interest in international affairs. De Valera had major involvement in the League of Nations in the 1930s, but in general Ireland had been inward looking until the 1950s. This card was issued in 1995 by An Post to commemorate fifty years of the United Nations. By implication, it also celebrates Ireland's role in the organisation. The Republic's membership dated from late 1955. Prior to that Ireland's membership had been vetoed by the USSR, as it was seen as an ally of the Western powers.

Since the 1960s Irish participation in UN peacekeeping forces has been extensive. Its most noteworthy military involvement was in the Congo from 1960 to 1964, where over 6,000 Irish soldiers served and 26 were killed, and in UNIFIL, the United Nations Interim Force in Lebanon. This latter service, as illustrated, was still ongoing at the time this postcard was issued.

Irish military personnel played a major role in the UN supervision of Israeli withdrawal from Lebanon, and in the wider peacekeeping effort in the area between 1978 and 2001 at considerable cost, as 47 Irish servicemen were killed while on active service in this region. It is reasonable to see the Irish contribution to UN peacekeeping as their most significant foreign policy initiative since independence.

Obviously the postcard examples displayed in this chapter are inadequate in trying to trace the history of the Republic of Ireland from 1923 to the present. While it would be foolish in the extreme to claim that every relevant postcard has been found, one is reasonably confident in believing that even if that feat had been accomplished, the picture would still remain very far from complete. At best, one can argue that a restricted range of postcards during this period throw a glimmer of light on a number of political issues, mostly those of minority protest groups.

9

COMMEMORATING OUR PAST
1690–1916

Introduction

Commemorative issues could probably merit a book of their own. The greatest single problem lies in deciding what categories of material should be included. These could range through pictures of artefacts, photographs or even paintings of castles or other historic monuments, reconstructions or pictures of events, and similar paintings or photographs of major historical figures, or indeed even of towns and villages in the past.

For the purpose of this study, an arbitrary decision has been made to include samples of work with an Irish connection, which illustrate or commemorate only major historical events, or depict the figures involved in them.

Even within these limits, there is quite an extensive range from which to make a choice. Events commemorated in postcards stretch from, for example, the religious and political struggles of seventeenth-century Ireland to the 1916 Rising. People, as diverse as Lord Castlereagh and James Connolly, are also featured. In total, they add up to a whirlwind tour of Ireland's past.

A clear majority, although by no means all, of the cards featured in this chapter are not directly political in intent. In a handful of cases, it is impossible to tell whether cards were issued for mainly promotional or political reasons, although on the balance of probabilities they have been deemed political. Their content in all cases is certainly highly political. It would be a brave or foolish writer who would attempt to dismiss the political significance of the battle of the Boyne, Daniel O'Connell or the Land League.

Nevertheless, the commercial aspect of many of these cards is at least as important if not more important than the political character or featured event. Some of these cards have been issued as marketing devices or profit-making wares by museums or galleries. Examples selected for this work were issued by Downpatrick Museum, the Michael Davitt National Memorial Museum, the Tate Gallery and the Ulster Museum, to name but a few. In some cases, cards were issued specifically to accompany major exhibitions, such as the Ulster Museum's 'Kings in Conflict'.

This type of material was normally produced to appeal to a wider market than the professional historian, and some would tend to see it as belonging more properly to the heritage industry. As such this type of card would probably be of much greater interest to the man in the street than to the academic.

Notwithstanding the intentions of museum marketeers to be non-political, the commemorative material which they issue cannot be apolitical, although it may attempt successfully to be non-party political. The very decision to undertake or fund any commemoration, be it through a march, a display, the opening of a museum or the issue of postcards, is rooted in political values. Those who decide to commemorate a political event or movement, in the process of that decision, make a political decision about the significance of that which they choose to commemorate. There may well be other motives which they deem more important, but the political cannot rightly be excluded irrespective of their intentions.

* * * * *

In November 1688, William Prince of Orange staked his claim to the throne, when he landed in England, at the invitation of English aristocrats, who were alarmed by the pro-Catholic policy of King James II, and above all by the recent birth of a Catholic heir to the throne. Irish Protestants were already unnerved by the implementation of similar policies in Ireland by his viceroy, the Earl of Tyrconnell.

After the withdrawal to Dublin of their Protestant garrison on the viceroy's orders, the Protestant inhabitants of Derry were panic-stricken by a rumoured Catholic plot to massacre them. When an advance party of the Earl of Antrim's Redshanks, a Catholic force, approached the city, some if not all the Protestant occupants assumed that the instrument of their destruction was at hand.

Seizing the initiative, or in blind panic, one cannot say which, a group of young apprentice boys locked the gates against them (no. 9.1). It was a harbinger of the later siege (April–July 1689) which over the centuries has come to symbolise heroic Protestant resistance to a Catholic takeover in Ireland. This closing of the gates, the siege itself, and the relief of the city by the *Mountjoy* after it had broken the boom on the River Foyle are featured in at least three

The Shutting of the Gates of Derry by the Immortal Apprentice Boys

9.1

141

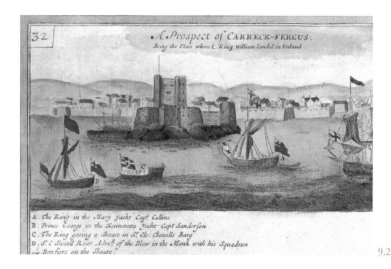

9.2

other cards in the 'No Surrender' series. There are several variations of the last mentioned from different publishers, and it forms a bedrock for loyalist culture.

This card is every bit as political as the modern Apprentice Boys annual commemoration service and march held in the city. The postmark reads September 1913 – dating it during the Home Rule crisis. Its clear political message stresses that, like their forefathers, modern unionists will remain firm in defending their interests.

Other cards issued for the tercentenary by the Ulster Museum, (nos. 9.2 and 9.3) show contemporary illustrations of the ensuing Williamite campaign in Ireland. Frederick, Duke of Schomberg, had captured Carrickfergus following a short siege in the late summer of 1689. The following June, William himself arrived on board

9.3

9.4

his yacht *Mary* (marked 'A' on no. 9.2). He was accompanied on his journey by his brother-in-law, Prince George of Denmark, and by a number of other dignitaries aboard the yacht *Henneretta*. The Prince of Orange went ashore on a smaller barge (marked 'C'), and was welcomed by the Mayor, the Corporation and representatives of the town's garrison. Having travelled through the town, William proceeded towards Belfast for a rendezvous with Schomberg. He then began his southerly advance towards Dublin. The Williamite and Jacobite armies clashed at the Boyne on 1st July (no. 9.3). Although it was neither the greatest military engagement nor even the most decisive engagement of the War of the Two Kings in Ireland, this has become the best-remembered battle of the whole campaign. John Killen, in his 1985 work on Ulster postcards, *John Bull's Famous Circus*, refers to two more overtly political cards of William crossing the Boyne.

Although it is true that the Boyne was not the most important military event of the war, it was the most important on a personal level for James. A rapid retreat to Dublin was followed soon afterwards by his final withdrawal from any part of the kingdoms he sought to regain. This is depicted in the painting 'Lost Cause' (later reproduced as a postcard for the Tate Gallery) by the Victorian artist Andrew Carrick Gow, where James is shown at a landing stage in Kinsale preparing to embark for exile in France (no. 9.4).

From almost the same period, and reflecting the aftermath of the Williamite Wars, comes this picture of Lady O'Neill, also known as Lady Molyneux (no. 9.5). Her father, Caryll, Third Viscount Maryborough (1622–99), was active in the Royalist cause during the English Civil War. His fortunes were subsequently restored under James II, who appointed him Lord Lieutenant of Lancaster. He remained loyal to James in 1688.

9.5

Frances married Sir Neil (or Niall) O'Neill. He was the son of Henry O'Neill of Shane's Castle, County Antrim and Eleanor (née Talbot), a sister of Richard Talbot, better-known by his later title, the Earl of Tyrconnell, who was appointed army commander in chief and viceroy in Ireland by James II.

With such a background it should come as no surprise that the O'Neills were loyal to James II. Neil himself raised a regiment of dragoons for James and is also known to have been present at the Siege of Derry in 1689. The following year, when William advanced to the Boyne, O'Neill commanded a detachment of troops at Rosnaree Ford. Here William's commander Schomberg was trying to cross so that he could outflank the Jacobite army. O'Neill was wounded in the fray, and died some days later following attempted surgery on his wounds.

The defeated in war can normally expect unpleasant repercussions. Lady O'Neill, having suffered the loss of her husband, now also had their estates confiscated in 1691. She was fortunate, however, that in 1700, she regained her property on appeal and survived until 1732.

Just three years before that, Edmund Burke was born (no. 9.6). He was to become one of the leading politicians of his time, some would say of any time. Burke was born into a Dublin legal family. After a spell in Trinity College, Dublin, he studied law at the Inner Temple in London, although he was never called to the Bar. In 1765 Burke became private secretary to the Whig grandee, Lord Rockingham, who soon became First Lord of the Treasury, or as we would now call it Prime Minister, of a short-lived government. As was customary at the time a parliamentary seat, representing Wendover, one of the pocket boroughs, was found for the young protégé. Having entered parliament in 1766, Burke rapidly established a reputation as a fine speaker.

In 1770, he supported parliamentary reform through the establishment of open parliamentary proceedings and the development of a proper party system to replace court influence. His pamphlet *Thoughts on the Cause of the Present Discontents* argued that although George III's attempts to exercise influence over the

Right Hon. Edmund Burke, M.P. 1729—1797.

9.6

government were legal according to the letter of the law, they were contrary to the spirit of the constitution.

By 1774, Edmund Burke had become a political ally of Charles James Fox. Conciliation of the American colonists, Irish commercial rights and religious toleration for Catholics were three major issues which he promoted. How different the history of USA, Britain and Ireland could have been had he met with greater success. Britain's colonial policy provoked a war with the American colonists, resulting in the loss of their colonies, and Burke's condemnation of Lord North's mismanagement helped bring about the latter's resignation in the spring of 1782.

Despite his importance to the Rockingham faction, Burke was never given a cabinet post. He had to settle for the more menial position of Paymaster to the Forces. Some have suggested that as an outsider Irishman, his face did not quite fit amongst the aristocratic Whigs. On the other hand, he was apparently difficult to work with. Fox, for example, called him 'a most unmanageable colleague'.

Burke continued his interest in another colony, India, and was the leading light in promoting the impeachment of Warren Hastings, who had been governor general from 1773 to 1784. The case dragged on for seven years until Hastings was eventually acquitted.

In its earliest stages the French Revolution was met with a fair amount of enthusiasm in Britain but Burke was quick to foresee inherent dangers. Alarmed by the abduction of King Louis XVI from Versailles to Paris in October 1789, Burke launched himself into what has become his best-known work, *Reflections on the Revolution in France*, which was published in November 1790. In this work, Burke argued that France would fall prey to arbitrary power. Although time was to prove Burke correct in his forecast, his stance was unpopular with some of the Whigs. By 1791 the long alliance of Fox and Burke was torn apart by their now conflicting views of the Revolution.

By 1793, Burke had thrown his support behind Pitt and the Tories, just as Britain went to war with France. In July of that year, Edmund Burke retired from parliament. He died some four years later, just a little too soon to witness a French inspired revolution within his country of birth.

Lord Edward
Fitzgerald

Born Oct. 15.1763
Died June 4.1798

THE IRISH STORE, NEW YORK.

He fought & bled
for his country cause
may his memory
always remain well
...

9.7

Burke's political philosophy is probably best summed up in the phrase, 'a liberty connected with order'. Although he has always traditionally been associated with the Whigs, he does not fit comfortably into any political party. At different times he was critical of the Tories as a threat to liberty and of the Whigs as a threat to order.

Burke had been supportive of reform in Ireland and would have been horrified, but not surprised when reformers such as the original United Irishmen became plotters of revolution from the mid-1790s. The Society was infiltrated with informers, and before they had the opportunity to put any plans into effect most of the leaders were arrested in March 1798. Lord Edward Fitzgerald alone escaped on this occasion.

His memory is commemorated in a rare American card published for the Irish Store in New York (no. 9.7). In accordance with American postal regulations, the address alone was written on the reverse. Lord Edward himself was seriously wounded during his arrest in May, and died a couple of weeks later. His arrest dealt a fatal blow to United Irish hopes and plans. He alone of all the leadership had some military experience, having served in the British Army during the American War of Independence. One can gauge for oneself whether this card is politically motivated or not. However, to judge from the correspondent's clearly legible comment on the front, and from one in a similar vein on another rather similar card depicting Napper Tandy, it clearly had some sort of political impact.

On Fitzgerald's arrest, the most important figures left on the United Irish executive were the Sheares brothers, John and Henry, both lawyers from Cork. Apparently there had been disagreement within the leadership on tactics for the planned rebellion. The brothers had argued for a rebellion starting in Dublin and then spreading outwards throughout the country. Others had supported the idea of revolts starting in outlying districts followed by an advance on Dublin. This was the plan adopted. Ironically when the Sheares brothers themselves were arrested only a day after Lord Edward Fitzgerald, it was a copy of their plans, which fell into the hands of the authorities. This caused the government some confusion as they expected a Dublin revolt, not that it made a lot of difference in the long run.

The Sheares were heavily influenced by the French Revolution. When they were arrested, one of them carried a proclamation in his own handwriting, which included the following statement: 'repair to the flag of liberty which is now flying. Many of the tyrants have already bled, many more will shortly bleed by decrees of the Revolutionary Tribunal which will be immediately established.'

No government could be expected to ignore such bloodcurdling threats. The brothers were executed and their bodies were taken to the crypt of St Michan's church, where they still lie (no. 9.8) Whether the intention in issuing this card was political or not is now impossible to say, but one might bear in mind the comment from Novick, that a mere cry of 'Remember '98' was in itself sufficient to wreck an army recruiting meeting during the First World War.

Antrim was one of the key centres in the United Irishmen's plans for a revolt in Ulster. Whatever qualities Henry Joy McCracken possessed, they were not those of a military strategist. The garrison in Antrim town has been estimated at about 150, but reinforcements could readily be sent from Belfast or Blaris, near Lisburn. No attempt appears to have been made to secure these routes against a government counter-attack.

Major-General Nugent, head of the army's northern command, had already been informed by an agent within the United Irishmen called Magin (or Mageean) of the impending revolt, and reinforcements were already en route, when McCracken assembled his force of at least 3,000 men on Donegore Hill. When they marched down into Antrim town on the afternoon of 9th June, they may have swollen to as many as double that number.

The defenders took up position in the castle grounds and market house at the bottom of the Main Street. Another force of United Irishmen, coming from Randalstown, attempted to attack the market house, but clashed with the first group of army reinforcements from Blaris. They had been driven back by McCracken's main force. In their retreat, these soldiers ran into the United Irish contingent coming from Randalstown.

The latter, inexperienced in warfare, broke ranks and scattered in the mistaken belief that they were under

1798.
THE BROTHERS JOHN & HENRY SHEARES

9.8

Who fears to speak of Ninety-eight ?
Who blushes at the name ?
When cowards mock the patriot's fate,
Who hangs his head for shame ?

He's all a knave or half a slave
Who slights his country thus ;
But a true man, like you man,
Will fill your glass with us.
(*J. K. Ingram.*)

THE BATTLE OF ANTRIM, 7th JUNE, 1798

9.9

attack. Further army reinforcements arrived with artillery, and the battle now became a rout. Up to 300 rebels were killed. Other inhabitants were killed indiscriminately in the mopping up operation. The battle was over within a few hours (no. 9.9).

The verse accompanying the artist's impression of the battle comes from the rebel song popularly known as, 'Who Fears to Speak of '98?' the author of which was the remarkable John Kells Ingram. In 1843, Ingram, a young Newry man, wrote these words for *The Nation*, the popular publication of the Young Irelanders. He subsequently became a professor and later still librarian in Trinity College, Dublin. He wrote a lot more scholarly works, all of them now comparatively obscure in comparison to these his early jottings.

An alternative version of this postcard (and of the following example) was issued by the Dungannon Club in 1907. It used the same artwork of the painter J.W. Carey (1859–1937), but it was combined with lines by the Ballymena-born poet, Ethna Carbery:

> And God be praised the pikes were red-before the sun went down
> And God be good to those who fell- that day in Antrim town.

There can be little doubt that this alternative version commemorating the battle is just as political, and arguably more overtly so, as the productions by the Dungannon Club. The wording on the version illustrated here may smack somewhat of alcohol-fuelled patriotism, but it is not difficult to see how it could be used to foment anti-British feeling.

After some initial successes, the rebels in County Down – under the leadership of Henry Munro – were routed at Ballynahinch on 13th of that same month. One of the rebel attacks was illustrated in a postcard issued by Baird of Belfast (no. 9.10).

THE BATTLE OF BALLYNAHINCH, FOUGHT 13TH JUNE, 1798; THE INSURGENTS, LED BY GENERAL MONRO, ATTACKING THE ROYAL FORCES UNDER GENERAL NUGENT.

9.10

With this defeat, the rebellion in Ulster was effectively over. By September it had also been crushed elsewhere, and the question soon arose as to how any re-occurrence could be prevented. It was at this point in time that Robert Stewart, Lord Castlereagh and later 2nd Marquess of Londonderry took centre stage (no. 9.11). As a young man he became MP for County Down, in which his home, Mount Stewart, was located. Now following the defeat of the rebels, as Chief Secretary for Ireland, his was a particularly important role. Contrary to the image of him which is sometimes portrayed, Castlereagh took a reasonably conciliatory approach towards the rebels. He issued, for example a proclamation offering pardon to all the rank and file rebels, who had joined the French invasion force in Connacht, provided they surrendered and handed in their arms.

LORD CASTLEREAGH.
PAINTING BY SIR THOMAS LAWRENCE.

Castlereagh's bad press amongst Irish nationalists rests on the fact that he, above all other contemporary politicians, was responsible for persuading the Irish parliament to vote itself out of existence. Castlereagh argued that an Act of Union was the best safeguard against the threat of another '98. In accomplishing his task of persuading the Irish MPs Castlereagh made extensive use of the then current means of political persuasion namely, patronage, sinecures, pensions and titles to guarantee a secure majority for the legislative union of Ireland and Britain.

9.11

149

Thomas Russell
1767–1803

9.12

In the years following the Union, Castlereagh held a variety of positions at Westminster. In 1812, he became Foreign Secretary, and in this position had the vital task of constructing yet another allied coalition against Napoleon. When at last this alliance defeated Bonaparte, Castlereagh played a prominent part in the reconstruction of Europe at the Congress of Vienna (1815), and to ensuring its security by the Quadruple Alliance of the same year. In 1822, he took his own life, during one of the periodic bouts of depression from which he had long suffered. This postcard is a copy of his portrait in the National Portrait Gallery.

Despite Castlereagh's success in achieving Union, political plotting was not ended. This picture of Thomas Russell, 'the man from God knows where', (no. 9.12) links the United Irishmen and Emmet's Rising of 1803.

As a close friend of the McCracken family and an active revolutionary, Russell was arrested in 1796. Internment in Scotland saved him temporarily from the fate of most of the rebel leaders. On his release, however, he involved himself in the plans of Robert Emmet, and this time his luck ran out. Following his arrest in 1803, Russell was convicted of high treason and was hanged outside Downpatrick Gaol, now renovated as Down County Museum, for whom this card was created.

9.13

ROBERT EMMET DELIVERING HIS FAMOUS SPEECH FROM THE DOCK, 19TH SEPTEMBER, 1803.
"Oh, my country, was it personal ambition that could influence me? Had it been the soul of my actions, could I not, by my education and fortune, by the rank and consideration of my family, have placed myself amongst the proudest of your oppressors? My country was my idol. To it I sacrificed every selfish, every endearing sentiment, and for it I now offer up myself, O God!"
(Robert Emmet.)

Robert Emmet (1778–1803) launched a futile, poorly organised, and poorly supported plan to attack Dublin Castle in July 1803. He had hoped that this would coincide with risings outside Dublin. At the earliest stage of his planning, he seemed to have also hoped for French help, but all his arrangements were thrown into chaos by an explosion at his arms dump in Patrick Street. The revolt, when it did take place, lasted only a couple of hours, although about fifty people were killed. For his part in this rising, Emmet was tried in September and executed.

9.14

This artist's impression of the trial (no. 9.13) is accompanied by a short extract from Emmet's speech from the dock. It is not the most quoted section, for which he is best remembered in republican circles: 'When my country takes her place among the nations of the earth, then and not till then, let my epitaph be written.'

A certain romance has been attached to Emmet because of his relationship with Sarah Curran, which probably led to his capture and death. Mystique has also been added by the fact that, despite several theories, no authenticated burial place has ever been identified.

This card is another clear example of an historical character being used to further political ends. The extract quoted from the trial speech is for some an unequivocal exhortation to self-sacrificing patriotism, an inspiration for later generations, one might conclude. For others it would constitute a malign incitement to further violence.

While some such as Emmet and Russell pursued their political views through violence, other chose the route of the constitutionalist. Of these, Daniel O'Connell, 'the Liberator' (1775–1847) is undoubtedly the most famous (no. 9.14). It is believed that this reproduction of O'Connell's signature and painting is part of a series issued in 1929 to commemorate the centenary of Catholic Emancipation. Whether it was meant to have any further political significance is unknown, although it could clearly have been of some use to the newly formed Fianna Fáil party, or even to the then current Cumann na nGaedheal in the Free State to stress the benefits of constitutional rather than violent republicanism.

Called to the Bar in 1798, O'Connell established himself as a successful advocate, before focusing his attention on politics. The Catholic Association (of

9.15

Ireland), which he co-founded in 1823, became a mass movement of real consequence the following year with the penny per month 'Catholic Rent'. Under pressure from this movement, whose supporters won a number of elections in the following years, the Prime Minister, the Duke of Wellington, and his Home Secretary, Sir Robert Peel, acting in the interests of public order, eventually conceded Catholic Emancipation in 1829. Early in 1830, O'Connell took his seat at Westminster, the first Catholic to sit there for centuries.

During the 1830s, O'Connell, often in alliance with the Whigs, promoted reform in Ireland, and supported a range of liberal causes, such as the abolition of slavery, parliamentary reform and the independence of Belgium.

In 1841, the Loyal National Repeal Association was launched, and O'Connell now became engaged in his second great crusade. According to O'Connell, 1843 was to be the year when repeal of the Act of Union would be won. A series of monster meetings drew large attendances, reportedly as high as a million. However, O'Connell's campaign won virtually no support in Britain and was adamantly resisted by Sir Robert Peel. Now Prime Minister, he was determined to stand firm against all O'Connell's threats and demonstrations. When Peel finally called his bluff, and forced the cancellation of his Clontarf meeting, O'Connell was a spent force.

Some, such as the Young Irelander, Thomas Francis Meagher, (no. 9.15), 'Meagher of the Sword,' were prepared to espouse violence, although O'Connell rejected all thoughts of this. The former became accordingly a hero of later physical force nationalists. The Great Famine dispelled any lingering hopes of success for the repeal movement either through violence or constitutional means. O'Connell died on his way to Rome in 1847. This postcard (no. 9.15) gives quite a good potted biography of Meagher.

Eviction scene 1879

The evicted

Tilling the land

Davitt Museum

Céad Mile Fáilte

9.16

The land question was the other great issue of the nineteenth century. Two factors had made the problem more acute. Until the Famine, the population had been growing rapidly, and the pattern of land tenure was changing to the detriment of the tenant. Landlords were replacing leaseholds with annual tenancies, permitting them to raise the rent each year and to leave tenants with little security of tenure. O'Connell had argued that land reform would naturally follow repeal. After his death agrarian reformers like James Fintan Lalor tried to keep this issue live for a while, but it was some thirty years later before any real progress could be seen.

This modern card published by the Michael Davitt Memorial Museum, Straide, County Mayo, commemorates the beginning of change (no. 9.16). The Land League of Mayo was founded by Michael Davitt and others. It developed rapidly, becoming the (Irish National) Land League in 1879. With the possible exceptions of O'Connell's Catholic Association and the Orange Order, it was to be the most important political mass movement in nineteenth-century Ireland. Although it is not the case in this instance, pictures of evictions as shown here and on other postcards, were used as part of separatists' anti-British argument.

The Land League's political clout was increased when Parnell, the leading nationalist politician of his day assumed the presidency. Although the movement had amongst its aims the complete abolition of the landlord class, its main purpose for many was the extension of the Ulster Custom throughout Ireland. These rights were the famous '3Fs' of Fair Rent, Free Sale and Fixity of Tenure.

Although the League espoused the force of argument rather than the argument of force, some violence was probably inevitable, given the depths of feeling about agrarian grievances, and the movement's strong links with Fenianism. Nevertheless, its chief and most effective weapon was the boycott, which Parnell recommended from 1880.

Separation from England would
be valueless unless it put the
people - the actual people and
not merely certain rich men -
of Ireland in effectual ownership
and possession of the soil of Ireland.
Padraic Pearse
1879 - 1916

by Padder

9.17

The greatest short-term gain of the League was Gladstone's Land Act of 1881. In effect, it granted the '3Fs', but those most in need, namely tenants in arrears of rent, were excluded from its provisions. Although this Act was only a beginning, it sounded the death-knell for landlordism in Ireland.

The twin issues of physical force and land ownership emerged again in the 1916 Rising. It is evident that the rebels of 1916 supported violence. Their attitudes to the land question are not always quite so obvious. Both standpoints are clearly highlighted in these modern cheaply produced cards (nos 9.17 and 9.18), issued by the Patriot Press Workers Co-op. Their political viewpoint needs no further explanation.

To my mind an agitation to attain a political or
economic end must rest upon an implied
willingness and ability to use force. Without that
it is mere wind and attitudinizing.
-James Connolly
1868 - 1916

9.18

And finally, this portrait (no. 9.19) of Constance Gore-Booth, better known as Countess Markievicz, was reproduced in 1968, along with one of James Connolly to commemorate the centenary of their births. Constance Markievicz was one of the most colourful characters of her time. In her thirties, she became a supporter of Sinn Féin, and was a co-founder of Fianna Éireann, the republican youth movement. During the Dublin Lockout of 1913, she worked closely with Connolly, and ran a workers' soup kitchen from Liberty Hall. As a member of the Citizen Army, she was second in command at Stephen's Green during the Easter Rising.

Following the rebellion, her death sentence was commuted, and in 1918, she became the first woman elected to Westminster. Of course, she refused to take her seat in accordance with Sinn

9.19

Féin policy. She was later appointed Minister of Labour in the First Dáil. Her opposition to the Treaty was vehement and her support for the Irregulars during the Civil War saw her back in prison. She was elected to the Dáil, but once again remained an abstentionist. She would not sit in the Free State assembly, which she refused to recognise. Constance Markievicz died in 1927 in a public ward of Sir Patrick Dun's Hospital. The circumstances of her death were not what one might have expected from her privileged background and upbringing, but they were in keeping with the life she had led and the company she had kept.

To sum up, this chapter gives no more than a taste of what is available. Some of the material is purely commemorative. However, much of it is most obviously politically motivated, drawing on quotation, both real and literary, and on historical events, to encourage continued involvement and support for a political cause. On balance there would appear to be much more nationalist than unionist-orientated material of this type.

REVIEW

How then should we sum up the usefulness of these postcards for the publishers, for those with political interests and motivation, and lastly, but not least for the historian both amateur and professional? There are considerable difficulties in trying to categorise the different types of material produced in the last century or so, but there is a broad spectrum of postcards ranging from those that featured political personages or events, but which in themselves were politically neutral, through to the out-and-out propagandist.

Commemorative political postcard material in the narrowest sense simply recalls and pictures important people or events from the past. Often the intentions of the publishers are purely commercial not political. They seek to promote their exhibition or their museum, and in so doing to raise some funds by the sale of relevant selected images. It is a perfectly reasonable and acceptable practice. These cards are numerous and there is no valid reason why history should not be saleable.

These cards differ from the majority featured in this work, in that they are secondary rather than primary material. In other respects there is no essential difference between them in their use of political events on cards, and contemporary cards issued for commercial purposes, by international publishers like Valentine's, national printers and photographers like Baird or Hely's, or small local enterprises.

To the professional historian, however, these commemorative cards are of limited interest, and are usually of minimal value for research purposes. They are more to be seen as stimulus material, namely that which will stimulate an interest, and in some cases, encourage further study into aspects of the past. As such, they should be seen as an *aperitif* in preparation for the heartier fare of the academic historian. Although they can play no more than a tiny cameo role in a work such as this, they cannot be dismissed out of hand.

To commemorate an event is frequently taken to include its celebration, and here we move into a more directly political motivation. Cards such as those in chapter 9, which celebrate events like the Siege of Derry and its outcome, and there are quite a number of this ilk, or the 1798 Rebellion – once again a popular subject, are very often much more than a mere remembering of battles past. They are quoted as encouragement for battles present, real or metaphorical, be they resistance to Home Rule or support for advanced nationalism. They may be narrow, blinkered and distorted in their appeals to loyalist/republican traditions and 'culture', but it is difficult to ignore their influence.

For convenience one tends to classify the remaining majority of cards, which deal with contemporary events, into two broad, but not watertight subdivisions.

The first of these we might call 'illustrative'. This category would encompass the majority of those cards shown in chapter 1, i.e. the comprehensive range of photographs of the Belfast Strike of 1907. These appear objective and have obvious narrative value. They offer breadth in their coverage of events and obviously supplement written source material. On the other hand they are somewhat lacking in depth when seeking to analyse the issue. This category of cards also includes photographs of political leaders and important events, samples of which can be found in chapters 2, 7, 8 and 9. This type of card was issued because there was clear public interest in major events such as strikes, demonstrations and disasters. On occasions, this type of material is also a useful source of information on social history such as dress and modes of transport.

Slightly different, although still included in this general 'illustrative' classification, are those cards in chapter 4, selected from the extensive range depicting the destruction in Dublin after the 1916 Rising. These were photographed primarily for commercial purposes and in their original state were politically neutral. If anything, the *Daily Sketch* would have been expected to reflect a government viewpoint, although that is not easily discerned in their work. Helys, the main Irish publishers of this type of material, may have had some sympathy for the rebels, but were first and foremost, a major commercial organisation, who would not wish to risk government wrath, whatever their private view might have been. They were dependant on government work and received commissions from government sources, such as the printing of early recruiting posters. However, we do know for certain that these pictures of Dublin in ruins were subsequently exploited by advanced nationalists in their attacks on British policies in Ireland.

Other cards in chapters 4, 6 or 7, whether photographs or artists' sketches, featuring dead or imprisoned rebels from 1916, 1919–21, or hunger strikers from 1981, clearly fit into the second category of 'propaganda' cards. A small minority may be simply and solely genuine memorials, but captions such as 'Died for Ireland' or 'Murdered by the British' reveal political motivation. Finally, the most obviously and blatantly political cards show verse, artists' impressions, cartoons and political murals. These make up most of the cards. A few appear in every chapter of the book, but are most commonly seen in chapters 2, 3 and 5.

Individual cards or small clusters of cards deal with disparate political campaigns like the threat of nuclear power to Ireland, and the lack of tourist development (chapter 8) or the inadequacy of funding for childcare in Northern Ireland (Con. no. 9) but the vast majority of all the cards produced are concentrated on three major topics, namely:

The Home Rule Bill, 1912 – chapter 2.
War and Revolution in Ireland 1914–23 – chapters 3, 4, 5 and 6.
Troubles in Northern Ireland post 1969 – mainly chapter 7.

Without any huge distortion one could even distil the bulk of them into a single issue, the Irish constitutional question, which also features, on a couple of occasions in chapter 1, and frequently in chapters 8 and 9. For the purpose of this overview we will examine some common features before looking briefly at how each major topic is presented.

* * * * *

All these cards have been labelled as propagandist, a term which we should try to define. Novick has pointed out that there is no single agreed definition of the term. However, one that would be widely acceptable will serve us as a working definition. Most would recognise political propaganda as the spreading of a message, aiming to appeal to the emotions and/or intellect, so as to influence attitudes and the subsequent actions of the widest target audience possible. Without exception, these cards do two things. They reflect in the first instance, the opinions, emotions and rationale of their promoters. It is believed that they also reflect a slice of contemporary opinion, which they also seek to reinforce and maximise in promoting their cause. More than the written word in many cases, images produced in these cards can capture the atmosphere of their times, and effectively, in some cases at least, transmit most effectively some of the passion of the cause being argued. The fact that many were produced in colour probably added to their impact, especially in the earlier years when colour reproduction was less widespread than it has become in the last few decades.

One general phenomenon noted in all three of our major subjects is that the greatest production of postcards comes from or on behalf of those who perceive themselves to be the underdogs. This is predictable because the political postcard most often exists as a medium of protest. Those who felt they had the greatest grievance produced the most. Thus unionists from around 1911 saw themselves as outnumbered and isolated, while facing the juggernaut of British government policy, in alliance with the Redmondites, the largest single political party in Ireland. Irish separatists after 1914 saw themselves opposing the might of the British Empire's war effort, again a policy, which was supported by the majority political party. Between 1916 and 1918 Sinn Féin remained the outsiders challenging, with increasing confidence, the established Parliamentary Party. Similarly, after 1969, postcard evidence would suggest that republicans often donned the mantle of victimhood as poor imprisoned second class citizens of Northern Ireland.

In all these cases, there was a less numerous counter-propaganda postcard campaign. Pro-war Irish recruiting posters were omnipresent, an estimated 1.8 million of them in total, but corresponding postcard production was nowhere of the same order. Post 1969, Northern Ireland unionists did produce cards in fairly sizeable numbers. There were exceptions, but they often defined themselves in reactive rather than proactive terms in defending their heritage against the republican threat. Unlike unionist cards from the 1912 era, they do not spell out their rationale to any noticeable degree.

Regarding each of our major political postcard topics, three questions in particular spring to mind. What type of propagandist content did they contain? What were the specific aims of their postcards and, by far the most difficult question, how effective was their postcard campaign?

Between 1911 and 1914 in particular Ulster unionists set out to oppose Home Rule by 'all means possible'. Postcards constituted a large element within that broader campaign of demonstrations, military organisation and publicity. In their postcards, they used just about every imaginable source – photographic material, verse old and new, original artwork, songs and cartoons. In tone they were often logical and well-argued, thus leaving us a clear idea of the motivation underlying their activities. They were sometimes comic, sometimes threatening, but almost always underpinned by a deep sense of insecurity and betrayal. They had a receptive audience. Any sort of propaganda campaign which highlighted those fears stood a reasonable chance of success.

In an age predating opinion polls, marketing surveys and the like, it is virtually impossible to measure in any objective way the impact of any propaganda campaign. All one can say with certainty as an initial assessment, was that the unionist campaign reflected major popular concerns and that the broader campaign itself was essentially successful. Postcards were available in huge numbers as a cheap, popular and readily accessible means to further their cause.

One attempt at analysis of propaganda by the Institute for Propaganda Analysis, may take us a couple of steps further in trying to assess its effectiveness in Irish postcards. The Institute examined the specific content of strategies which were the mark of successful propaganda campaigns. Key components, some of which require little or no further explanation, were identified and entitled as follows:

Name Calling – Give a dog a bad name!
Generality – Association of one's cause with something good, which they
    entitled – a 'virtue word'.
Transfer – Linking one's case to something respected, or one's opponent to
    something disrespected.
Testimonial – Support from the famous.
Plain Folks – Association of one's own ideas with ordinary people.
Cardstacking – Selective use (or distortion?) of facts to build a case against
    opponents.
Band Wagon – An encouragement to join the 'winning side'.

It is not being suggested that this in a template for every successful propaganda campaign, but there are common features, and we can note a close correlation between these strategies and many of our postcards.

How for example do the unionists present themselves particularly in their anti-Home Rule campaign? In this representative postcard selection, they are constantly depicted as a brave, resolute God-fearing virtuous race of men, women and children, who have remained loyal to their traditions, and who have proven through the ages that they will not be subdued, from the defiance of the Apprentice Boys, who showed themselves prepared to stand up against a threatening army in December 1688, to the UVF gun-running of April 1914. Their loyalty and virtue has been shown to be rewarded with the support and blessing of the great and the good from the aristocracy, such as Earl Spencer and Lord Salisbury, to the leaders of the Conservative Party, Chief Secretary for Ireland especially Bonar Law, of the army and the church. Some of these traditional defenders of the law are even prepared to support violence such is the perceived rightness of the cause to which they have given their testimonial.

This people are shown as united, irrespective of class in their quest to stop the 'Home Rule Conspiracy'. There are in fact two contrasting cards entitled 'The Plot that Failed' and 'The Plot That Did *Not* Fail.' comparing the Liberal-Redmondite Home Rule policy with the UVF gun-running. Mass support ('the Band Wagon') is demonstrated through their frequently photographed marches, their drilling, the signing of the Covenant and a series of massed rallies. More were encouraged to back the 'Winning Hand', (even featured on a card entitled 'The Red Hand and the Winning Hand'), as the gun-running had made them more powerful, and the agencies of the state namely the RIC, floundered helplessly and comically in search of their arms.

This brave tribe is shown facing a dangerous and cunning enemy, which is also labelled as cowardly when in the form of a fox it flees pursued by Ulster's defender. The leader of the conspiracy is devious, advertising Home Rule, while plotting separation. He threatens freedom in alliance with a scheming clergy, and can offer only a poverty-stricken future.

It almost goes without saying that of course the unionist propagandists exaggerated in their cards the threats to their financial, political and religious well-being, as shown best in images of various Ulster towns under Home Rule. It is as good an example of 'Cardstacking' as one is ever likely to find.

Of course, this does not offer proof of the effectiveness of the unionist postcard campaign, but it does stretch credibility to argue that this wealth of material which is clearly in tune with well-documented unionist fears and attitudes, and which conforms to a very large degree, to attested success criteria had little impact.

An analysis of Irish separatist propaganda between 1914 and 1921 would point towards a similar conclusion. In their cards and other propaganda, they opposed enlistment, condemned British brutality and ruthlessness in Ireland from the 1916 Rising onwards, and attacked the Irish Parliamentary Party for its support of the British war effort, and consistently labelled its leadership as mercenary.

In the later years, 1917 and 1918, as the separatist position strengthened, there was a clear attempt to challenge the Redmondites electorally. Opposition to enlistment appeared in postcards as a key issue. Clearly this resonated with the fears of many Irish families for the safety of their loved ones. As the casualties of war grew in number, resistance to recruitment grew on a European-wide basis. With the exception of the final months of war, there is a clearly established reduction in Irish recruitment between 1914 and 1918. Self-preservation was probably a much stronger motivation for this trend than any propaganda campaign.

This may appear to undermine the case for the effectiveness of separatist propaganda. That is not so. Given the prevailing public mood, Sinn Féin, the party which most obviously and consistently opposed all enlistment, never mind the more recently mooted conscription, was the party most likely to benefit in terms of increasing support, which was shown eventually in electoral terms. Its policy as presented in postcard form, was in marked contrast to the IPP, who had consistently supported enlistment. In other words the postcard propaganda acted as a very efficient catalyst in the moulding of political opinion.

Sinn Féin promoted itself with 'Virtue Words'. Its supporters depicted themselves as brave forthright promoters of 'The People's Rights' and also as too astute to fall for British blandishment such as the offer of Home Rule. Their weak, effete, sycophantic rivals in the Parliamentary Party are shown again and again in contrast as motivated by the pecuniary advantage of parliamentary service rather than any patriotic desire to serve Irish needs.

They are condemned by clergy, for example Bishop O'Dwyer. They are labelled as 'Dastards,' 'Felon Setters,' 'Traitors,' and 'Snakes' by patriots of old like Wolfe Tone but also by their contemporary rivals Sinn Féin. Even supposed allies like Asquith are now shown discarding Redmond disdainfully as a 'Scab.'

With their top hats, their greed and their best 'West Britons' accents, they may defend the 'Pawty' but they are far removed from the 'Plain People' of Ireland, who are shown as 'Unconquerable' like the Irish-Irelander both Gaelic and proud. In contrast, the Redmondites are shown as ready to send their fellow Irishmen abroad to fight and die in Britain's war. Irish separatists sacrifice themselves, and die at home as martyrs at British hands, to be mourned by real Irish patriots as shown in their numerous memorial cards.

And yet these poor deluded parliamentarians, if only they could stop their prevarication in the futile Convention, and listen to the reasonable pleas of Sinn Féin, one more push combined with the new mass movement ('Band Wagon') of the people of Ireland, they would achieve the independence which was just within their grasp.

When the political slide of the Parliamentary Party is confirmed by the 1917–18 by-elections, Gordon Brewster emerged again to encourage still more people to join the political 'Band Wagon' in his 'Party on the Rocks.' It is not the most praiseworthy of human traits to kick an opponent when down but it is a real one nevertheless, and it is well-established that human nature is such, that we normally want to associate with the successful. By the December 1918 election Sinn Féin had become the obvious political victors in Ireland.

Censorship is one rather important side issue, which needs to be addressed regarding the effectiveness of postcards published from the start of the First World War. It affected all published material but Novick has pointed out that postal censorship was much more thorough than other varieties. DORA was used between 1914 to control all material but postcards had an additional, inherent weakness.

Common sense dictates that posting makes propaganda much more vulnerable. Channelling material through a central point such as a major post office or sorting office makes it easier to operate a system of censorship. Any sort of sedition on a posted card is even more easily spotted than in a letter, and it carries also the obvious risk that it will identify the recipient and their address to the authorities. (There is a small amount of evidence to suggest that on occasions cards may have been sent in sealed envelopes in an attempt to circumvent this problem.) Does that then minimise the effectiveness of spreading a political message in postcards? Certainly not to the extent that one might think, for a number of reasons.

In the first instance, although this applies to a minority of cards, what are normally referred to as 'postcards', are not in every case meant to be posted. A few, which in all cases, do not even include a box for the stamp, were primarily designed and sold as fundraisers. Examples, and they probably do not tell us the whole story, include 'With Compliments From The Irish Brigade', in support of the Employment Bureau for Disabled Irish Soldiers and Sailors, Dublin, William Conor's cards in aid of the UVF Hospital at Shaftesbury Square, Belfast, and a picture of the rebels Daly, Clarke and Mac Diarmada, which raised funds for the Irish National Aid and Volunteer Dependents' Fund.

Secondly, and this probably extends to a much greater number of cards, they were often sold in sets as collectors' items. As stated previously, the first couple of decades of the twentieth century constituted the 'Golden Age' of postcards. Overall in this period a large proportion of all cards are 'postally unused'. The hobby of collecting postcards more than anything else has helped ensure their survival for the past century. The percentage of unused as opposed to 'postally used' Irish separatist cards which the writer has seen comes close to 100 per cent.

Finally, there is some evidence that cards could have circulated well-beyond the purchaser even when not posted. It is believed that cards were not simply stored away, but that they were shown to those who could be trusted, were passed around and discussed. There is specific evidence that this applied to other types of written material, and there seems little reason to doubt that it applied to postcards also. In addition, postcards have a marginal advantage over leaflets and pamphlets in that their being made of card lends a slightly greater durability to them over paper ephemera. It has also been observed that there was a considerable crossover between media, between for example, papers, posters and cards. Most commonly, a cartoon was published and was later issued as a postcard to spread its appeal.

The most recent significant issue of cards pertains to the post 1969 Troubles. Nobody can say with certainty how many of these exist, but a reasonable estimate, excluding copious election literature in the form of postcards from a range of political parties, is about 200. The larger proportion of these would be republican or at least anti-government in tone. Nevertheless, they also include a substantial number of loyalist cards, probably in excess of 50. They are narrow in scope, the bulk of them displaying their murals, mostly located in Belfast. They were produced by or for groups such as the UDA, although only very few state this specifically.

The anti-government cards fall into two main groups. The smaller of these, consisting of some 30 cards (most of them listed by Killen) were issued directly by the republican movement. Many of them carry a caption either 'Revolutionary greetings from Ireland.' or 'The British way of life in Ireland'. One would expect them to be promoting the notion of a united Ireland. While that is certainly implicit, it is not immediately obvious from a look at the pictures. Most of these stick to one of two themes. Either they show rioting in progress or the Provisional IRA on 'active service.' All appear to date from the early 1980s, and some carry the identical and explicit message from Bobby Sands on the reverse:

> There can never be peace in Ireland until the foreign, oppressive British presence is removed, leaving all the Irish peoples as a unit to control their own affairs and determine their own destinies as a sovereign people, free in mind and body, separate and distinct physically, culturally and economically.

The second cluster of cards was issued in criticism of government policy in Northern Ireland. Most, but by no means all, emanate from within Northern Ireland. Many serve a fundraising as well as a propagandist purpose. Sometimes it is quite difficult to determine which function takes priority. Certainly the percentage of these modern cards which serve a fundraising purpose is much higher than it ever was in any of the earlier postcards. Cards were issued by Green Cross to help epublican prisoners' families, by Just Books in aid of the Prisoners Books Scheme, Pat Finucane Centre, Bloody Sunday Initiative and the Bloody Sunday Justice Campaign. The last three groupings shared the same address.

While they may well not be all-embracing, six topics would summarise the content of a very high proportion of all the anti-government cards. These are rioting, commemoration of 'fallen heroes', Bloody Sunday 1972, prisoners in general and the Hunger Strikes of 1981 in particular, rubber/plastic bullets, and criticism of security forces with special reference to collusion between those security forces and loyalist paramilitaries.

As in the other major subjects of postcard production, the question arises as to how well the issues raised resonated with the target audience. It is not immediately obvious what that audience was. Rather tentatively one would take it as being nationalist Ireland in the broadest sense along with sympathisers abroad.

Although the Republican movement would have seen itself as fighting a political and military campaign for a united Ireland, the Troubles were more often presented in postcards as a human rights or series of human rights issues. There is some objective evidence that at least part of its target audience saw events in that light also. Staunton, in his study of Northern Ireland nationalists, for example, reported on a participant observation study in Ardoyne in the late 1970s. Here the IRA campaign was seen as 'a civil rights war expressed in national liberation terms' (Staunton, *The Nationalists of Northern Ireland*, p. 282).

There is little argument that, Bloody Sunday and the Hunger Strikes seriously disturbed nationalist Ireland in the broadest sense and won sympathy for republicans well-beyond their core support. They were therefore undoubtedly good topics for republicans to use to promote their cause. They helped turn Catholic opinion anti-government at least, if not actually pro-IRA.

The effects of Bloody Sunday were hugely damaging to the government in boosting the fortunes of republicanism. A persistent campaign, some of it in postcard form, demanding a new inquiry to replace Widgery, eventually culminated in the government establishment of the Saville enquiry at a cost well in excess of £150 million. Governments do not normally spend that amount of money, unless they feel under serious pressure.

The Hunger Strike deaths were arguably the most emotive issue of the Troubles for the nationalist people of Ireland. The burning of the British Embassy in Dublin, the Sands funeral, 'the largest since Parnell' (Staunton, *The Nationalists of Northern Ireland*, p. 278), the election of Owen Carron later in the year and the Sinn Féin victory in the West Belfast election of 1983 are some of the more obvious manifestations of its effects. Postcards illustrate support and sympathy for the hunger strikers but they show little of the political polarisation created by the strike in Northern Ireland.

Campaigns against rubber bullets and collusion issues are not as high profile and their importance for a wider nationalist community are accordingly not as easily established. However, the former, which features in at least six cards and the latter depicted in at least five, have been addressed by the British government with a restriction of their use and a search for alternative crowd control measures in the case of the former, and the Stevens, Stalker and other inquiries into collusion, examining the latter.

In the case of unionist anti-Home Rule cards and of the separatist material from 1914 onwards, there was an almost uncanny correspondence with the typical elements of successful campaigns as identified by the Institute for Propaganda Analysis. Postcards from the most recent conflict do not show anything like as strong a pattern, although one could clearly see evidence of 'Cardstacking' in their selection of topics, not just in what they say, but in what they omit.

A case has been made that republican postcards highlighted issues, most of which were of crucial importance to Irish nationalists and that their focus on these at least contributed to the increasing political influence of Sinn Féin. If republicans' key aim was Irish reunification then success was not, and realistically, could not be achieved through a postcard campaign. If on the other hand their key aim was to gain political, and by that we mean electoral strength, presumably as an interim step towards their ultimate goal, then success might just be claimed.

How significant has the use of politics in postcards been for political developments since 1969? It has already been observed how difficult it is to measure this sort of influence. The problem is compounded by the tsunami of mass media which has developed in the past half-century. The visual image through television and latterly the internet has acquired an importance, which challenges, and at the very least partly supersedes, the influence of all written and printed sources, although one is loath to deny the continuing influence of the cartoon.

It can be no coincidence that the governments of both Britain and the Irish Republic sought for years to deprive the Irish republicans of the oxygen of publicity by a form of television censorship. The printed word, including postcards, was largely ignored, arguably because it posed a much lesser threat.

Undoubtedly, both loyalists and nationalists have at different times made effective use of postcards to promote a political message. Loyalists could claim success in their opposition to Home Rule and separatist nationalists in their competition with the Irish Parliamentary Party. Postcards had some influence, but it would be foolish to see it as essential to their success. The influence of more modern cards is more problematical, but it is reasonable to conclude that, despite their reduced role, republicans did use them effectively to highlight issues which were important for the whole nationalist community and that this proved of electoral value to themselves.

CONCLUSION

Political postcards were just getting into their stride in the first decade of the twentieth century. Nevertheless, they did allude to key political issues, both looking backwards to the nineteenth century, and forward to those questions, which were of continued importance in the twentieth century. Political relationships within Ireland and tensions between Ireland and Britain, issues such as devolution, economic domination, trade union rights, women's rights and enlistment in the British armed forces all featured as themes.

Postcards were a substantial part of the anti-Home Rule movement, of the 1916 Rising for illustrative and propagandist purposes, and most importantly for the revival and renewal of Sinn Féin in its struggle with the Irish Parliamentary Party.

By the early 1920s, there was clearly a marked decline in the production of postcards. That phenomenon can be explained by the classic law of supply and demand, as several factors operated to shrink the market.

The censorship, which operated during the First World War, had some effect in reducing the number of cards issued, but the doubling of the postal charge from 1/2d to 1d in 1918 was probably much more significant. Some consider that the growth of alternative means of communication in the 1920s, particularly the telephone, also reduced the need to communicate by post. Greater mobility for an increasing number of people with the introduction of the motor car has also been quoted as a cause of decline, because more people could now visit friends and acquaintances, but this is not thought to have had such a great effect. Improved technology leading to a greater use of photographs may also have made a difference in increasing competition for 'real photo' cards. Finally 'Picture Postcard Values 2012', a catalogue for dealers and collectors, argues that the Great War had simply 'destroyed a national mood', and that people could no longer be bothered with the 'fripperies of the picture postcard'.

Postcards were still being produced in huge quantities, of course, but there is very little political material relating to Ireland. Apart from the broader picture, an additional factor relevant to Ireland also operated.

The great issues of the previous decade had been settled by 1923, at least for the present. In both parts of Ireland, the winners, Ulster Unionists in Northern Ireland and Cumann na nGaedhael in the Free State, quietly consolidated their victory, while the losers licked their wounds. No longer would propaganda be either necessary or effective.

* * * * *

From this limited selection of postcards alone, it should be clear that they can open a window on Irish history. Although they do not furnish us with a large amount of new information, they do illuminate the past, and frequently indicate vividly the opinions and attitudes of people, who lived in other times. Sometimes their humour is laboured and their views may infuriate. The past is used time and again to justify their present standpoint, and their attitude is often narrow and backward looking. Despite all this, they offer a panoramic, if somewhat predictable sketch of Irish history from the seventeenth to the late twentieth century.

Although their limitations must be recognised, it would be a gross error to completely dismiss the significance of political postcards. They can have an immediacy and pithiness often absent from the written word. The pictorial medium is well suited to deliver a clearly understood direct message. The value of humour is recognised by the designers of many of the cards, something that would be well-understood by the modern advertising industry. At their best, cards not only present their central theme, but embellish their argument effectively.

At their weakest, cards are very simplistic and fail to rise above mere sloganising. Many of the cards tend to be repetitive and appear to the modern reader as lacking originality. They also, consequently, leave little scope for analysis. Yet repetition, while it might not engage a later historian, is sometimes far from being the weakness it might appear. An attempt at arguing with an advertising executive that repetitive promotion/propaganda is a deficiency would cut very little ice. In the political field, even a cursory examination of the work of archetypical propagandists such as Goebbels or Stalin, would reveal the great store they set on repetition.

One genuine problem for researchers is that some of the cards have tended to date badly. Their intelligibility depends to a great extent on a very considerable knowledge of minutiae to understand their context, and interpretation can accordingly be tricky. This difficulty is also increased by the fact that a very large proportion of cards have never been catalogued.

Con. 1

167

Con. 2

Without this or even a postmark to at least give a *terminus ante quem* (that is to provide a date before which the card was published), accurate dating is not possible in some cases.

One of the more interesting features of all these cards is the marked similarities displayed even in those promoting conflicting political viewpoints. They often use much the same devices, and draw upon a similar range of images to convey their message. Thus, there is not a great deal of difference between the romanticised maiden of nationalist Ireland (nos. 2.25, 2.26), the doggedly-determined Ulster heroine, who holds the pass alone against Home Rule, (no. 2.13), and the forthright 'Mother Ireland', who wields the Sinn Féin brush to sweep the British from Ireland's shores (no. 5.2).

In similar fashion, and in different eras, children were pressed into service. Their depiction ranges from the belligerent defiance of, 'Who says we're to have Home Rule?' (Conclusion 1), through the involvement of the young catapulter depicted

Con. 3

168

in some of the early street violence, (Conclusion 2), to the sometimes insidious influence of violence on children, as shown in some of the work of Christine Spengler (Conclusion 3). Interestingly, it took the work of an outsider to show that insight. For many years until rather recently, it has frequently reflected our normality.

Glorification or even virtual deification of the leadership is yet another common theme. The fallen hero in particular, is the subject of adulation (e.g. nos. 4.14, 7.15, 7.18 etc.). It is noteworthy that loyalists and republicans alike have utilised the self-same champion – the mythological Cúchulainn (Conclusion 4, 5 and 6). Pearse drew

Con. 4

on the image of the same hero in his poem 'Mise Éire' ('I am Ireland'). His statue, as the fallen leader, now stands in Dublin's GPO, the rebel headquarters, where it commemorates the Rising.

Con. 5

Con. 6

For loyalists, Cúchulainn, of Gaelic legend, is the champion of Ulster, which he had, according to that legend, defended single-handed against the invading hordes from Connacht. He is now likened in their mural to the present 'Champions of Ulster,' the loyalist prisoners of war (LPOW), who languish in jail for their cause.

Marches, rallies and drilling in support of divergent political philosophies, probably aimed at showing the strength of their following, are also commonly depicted (nos. 2.2, 2.3, 2.4, 4.1, Conclusion 7, etc.). It is not being facetious to note that one could build up a postcard collection of marchers alone, if one were

Con. 7

Con. 8

so minded. Flags or uniforms may differ, but the message is largely the same. The exact words may vary but 'We are the people' or 'We will not be moved' would be largely interchangeable captions for the vast majority of them.

It is this very lack of mobility, which has condemned Ireland, especially Northern Ireland, to continuing years of tragedy. Whatever the longer-term outcome of the relatively recent peace moves and structures of Government, and only a prophet could forecast stability with absolute confidence, there can be no doubt that flexibility on all sides will continue to be essential to reach a lasting accommodation on the Ulster Question. Forecasting that necessary movement would be about as accurate a definition of optimism as you are ever likely to find, and yet there has undoubtedly been change in the last few years. A clear majority has recognised the sterility of past attitudes, and some have even been prepared to campaign vigorously for a more conciliatory and hopeful future (Conclusion 8). An executive with shared powers constitutes major progress, although there is plenty of room for disagreement about how much has been achieved.

As we repeatedly stumble and stutter towards accommodation of sharply differing views, some conclusions have become unavoidable. Unsurprisingly, there has been and there remains a huge absence of trust between unionist and nationalist representatives. It is only by taking risks that a stronger working relationship can develop. Unfortunately there has been very little mileage in past attempts at compromise from 1912 onwards. No matter what is eventually agreed, it will take sustained effort and above all else more time, measured in years, and possibly even decades, to soften the bitterness fertilised by the events of the thirty odd years of the Troubles in Northern Ireland.

One further and final observation has to be made, that while postcards were often propagandist in the past, their use was far more widespread than that. They were often the only pictorial record of major events for many people. In more recent times, other media fulfil that role more effectively.

Irish political postcards are now used solely as a medium of protest by committed minorities or pressure groups, about, for example, partition, government inaction on a range of issues, the inadequacy of childcare provision (Conclusion 9), imperialism or the threat of nuclear disaster. Perhaps then the political postcard can continue to flourish, albeit in a greatly reduced role, for another century.

Con. 9

APPENDIX 1: ARTISTS

Note

The source of the postcards recorded in this appendix is indicated in brackets thus e.g., (**TCD**), etc. Where no such indication has been given, the cards have been located in private hands, although of course, some may also exist in public collections. Numbers in brackets indicate illustrations used in this text.

Abbreviations

INT	Internet, e.g., www.vintagepostcards.com/www.eBay.co.uk
LCM	LIMERICK CITY MUSEUM
LIN	LINEN HALL LIBRARY
NLI	NATIONAL LIBRARY OF IRELAND
TCD	TRINITY COLLEGE DUBLIN, Samuels Collection

Since the artists who designed most of the nationalist Irish political postcards from 1914 onwards were at best sailing very close to the wind with regard to their legality, it is not surprising that much of their work was anonymous. It seems fairly certain that it was for the same reason that some of the artists used pseudonyms or initials disguising their identities. Even before 1914, the producers of anti-Home Rule cards were often threatening, celebrating or recording illegality, such as the Larne gun-running, and so the same would apply to their work though perhaps to a slightly lesser degree.

John Killen's work, *John Bull's Famous Circus*, identified a sizeable number of the artists who produced the Ulster Home Rule cards. There is no intention to replicate here work already done. However, some additional information is offered below on both artists and photographers.

Bricriu: No biographical details could be found for the artist using this pseudonym, but it is an interesting choice. The cartoonist clearly had some knowledge of old Irish mythology. Bricriu was best known in a tale from the Ulster Cycle as a troublemaker par excellence. His star moment is captured in the tale 'Fledh Bricrend', when he set out brilliantly to provoke jealousy and dissension between Cúchulainn and others of the Red Branch Knights. The only example met of this cartoonist's work on a postcard was the 'Irish Anti-National Exhibition', which first appeared as a cartoon in *The Republic* on 28th March 1907, and was advertised for sale as a postcard a fortnight later (**1.7**).

Gordon Brewster, 1889–1946: He was the son of W.T. Brewster, General Manager of Independent Newspapers, for whom he worked from 1906. He trained in the Dublin Metropolitan School of Art and exhibited with the Royal Hibernian Academy in 1916 and 1917.

Gordon Brewster is also known to have worked as a cartoonist before and after 1920 for the *Irish Weekly Independent* and also briefly for the comic journal *Quiz*. His cartoons for the *Sunday Independent* appeared under the title 'This, that and the other'. He was apparently much in demand by commercial firms and produced numerous postcards after 1916 of a generally pro-Sinn Féin character. He designed these cards for the Dublin firms of O Hanrahan's, North Circular Road, J.J. Walsh, Blessington Street and under the logo 'GHB', presumably acting on his own behalf as both artist and producer. They include the following:

> To Freedom
> To The Dead Of Easter Week 1916 (**LCM**)
> Chorus of Dillon and Devlin – 'Think of the Pawty, John' (**5.10**)
> Sinn Féin The People's Rights (**5.1**)
> Making A Clean Sweep Of It (**5.2**)
> Run Away Home to Your Foster-Mother, Johnny (**5.3**)
> The Party On The Rocks (**5.6**)
> The Last Of The Snakes (**5.8**)
> Following in Father's Footsteps (**5.11**)
> The Dangling Carrot (**NLI**)
> If (**5.13**)
> I'm Afraid I'll Have To Drop My Parcel (**TCD**)
> The Real 'Rainbow Chaser' (**INT**)
> Easter 1918 'Be Ye Faithful Unto Death' (**LCM**)
> Forcible Feeding (**TCD**)
> The Only Remedy (**TCD**)
> Peace Conference (Empty Chair at Versailles) (**TCD**)
> 'The Will of The People' 'Nigger Chiefs Deciding Their Form of Government'
>   (**TCD**)
> PAT I'll Have The Same Measure As My Friend Here (**5.16**)
> 1919 House of Commons during an Irish Debate (**6.1**)
> The Gun To Rule The Day (**LCM**) (**6.13**)

Thomas Fitzpatrick, 1860–1912: Fitzpatrick, who signed his work with his surname or the abbreviated 'Fitz', and who also worked under the pseudonym 'Spot' for *The Nation*, was born in Cork and worked for a couple of years in the 1880s as chief cartoonist for *Pat*. This magazine counteracted the crude stereotyping of Irishmen, particularly by the likes of Kenny Meadows and Tenniel in *Punch*. He had a particular dislike of 'Paddy' jokes. According to Snoddy, he also depicted the failings of John Redmond in his work. He never really forgave Redmond for his consistent support of Parnell after the party split over the O'Shea case.

Fitzpatrick worked for other magazines, such as the *National Press*, *Irish Emerald* and *Weekly Nation*, before founding his own humorous revue, *The Lepracaun* [sic], which existed from 1905 until 1915. A book of his cartoons from its first year was published in 1913.

Two, at least, of his numerous cartoons appeared as postcards and are included in this work.

> 'In the Old Days' (**LCM**) (**1.5**)
> 'Alas! My poor Brother' Dublin Castle Jewel Mystery (**1.6**)

Rowel Friers, 1920–98: He was born in Belfast and was an extremely talented cartoonist and illustrator. Amongst those for whom he worked were *London Opinion*, *PTQ*, *Dublin Opinion*, *Belfast Telegraph*, *Irish Times*, *Irish Press*, *Irish Independent* and *The Daily Express*. He also designed for amateur theatre and for the Lyric Theatre, Belfast, as well as publishing several books of cartoons. Friers had a keen eye for observing many of the absurdities of the Northern Ireland Troubles. A single example of his work appears in this book. Most of his work was confined to newspapers as opposed to postcards but these examples are known.

> 'It's A Little Souvenir I Bought From Dublin Dear.' (7. 5)
> Orange Drummers (Doing The Lambeth Walk). [This title appears in hand printed form.] (**LIN**)

Ernest Kavanagh, 1884–1916: Kavanagh, who was from Dublin, worked as a clerk, and was a cartoonist for *The Irish Worker* (1911–15). He was killed in the vicinity of Liberty Hall during the Easter Rising. At least four of his cartoons appeared as postcards.

> Asquith. Like all Scabs, Redmond, you are a failure from a business standpoint. (5.4)
> Shade of Wolfe Tone: Dastards, Traitors and Felon-Setters. (5.5)
> The Nation Mutilated (Redmond and Carson 1914)
> The Angel of Freedom

Donald McGill, 1875–1962: This famous London-born graphic artist is sometimes known as 'the King of the smutty postcard'. His favourite themes, heavy with *double entendre* depicted newly-weds, courting couples, predatory males and nubile young ladies, etc., but his work also included social observation, at least ten First World War series, varying from the comic to recruitment material, and half a dozen cards on Irish Home Rule. Two of these touch on his most common themes, sex and the henpecked husband. Although one of these cards, which links two contemporary issues, namely the demand for votes for women and Home Rule, is unsigned, both the style and even more tellingly the sequence number leave no room for doubt, that it is McGill's work. One estimate claims that 200,000,000 of his cards were issued during his lengthy career.

His Home Rule cards were as follows:

> Phwat! You talk about being a Home Ruler whoile oi'm aloive (A 311)
> A Real Home Ruler (A 312)
> Arrah Now The Bhoys 'LL Niver Refuse Us The Vote Whin They Git A
>   Parlymint Of Their Own! (A 313)
> unsigned
> Bedad, I Don't Care What Feller's M.P. So Long As This Feller Aint M.T. (A 314)
> 'An Act Of Union' Which Satisfies Both Parties (A 315) (**2.32**)
> An Orangeman In Ulster (A 316)

George Joseph Monks, 1879–[?]: This cartoonist was identified by Novick as the artist responsible for anti-conscription cards during the First World War, but few biographical details could be traced. He was born in Dublin in 1879 and was an illustrator in the boys' magazine *Our Boys*. It was published by the Educational Company of Ireland along with the Irish Christian Brothers. His work is unsigned, but he sometimes uses a small dog as an icon in the cartoons. Postcards attributed to him were:

> The First Irish Conscript
> Mobilising an Irish Conscript (The Second Irish Conscript) (**3.11**)
> Third Irish Conscript (In The Coffin)
> Gentle D.O.R.A. (**3.13**)

Others believed to be this artist's work include:

> Drilling An Irish Conscript (**3.12**)
> Small Boy – 'Hey! Mister. d'ye you know there's a back way in your place?'

Jack Morrow, 1872–1926: John Cassell Morrow, normally known as Jack, was one of eight brothers, at least six of whom were artists of some sort or another. He was born in Hanover House, Clifton Street, Belfast. Morrow became a landscape painter and political cartoonist as well as working for the Ulster Literary Theatre. John Killen attributed two political postcards in the Dungannon Club series to this artist, namely, 'Catching Recruits,' and 'The Secret of England's Greatness'. The latter is unsigned. Morrow used a variety of signatures on his work including 'J M, Seaghan' or 'Sean Mac Murchadha'*, 'Mac' or 'Sean M'.

Morrow ran a painting and decorating business in Dublin along with his brother Fred. By 1917 he was a politically active cartoonist. During 1917 and 1918, he published regular political cartoons in *New Ireland*. Quite a lot of his work appeared in postcard form. One could reasonably suspect that more postcards exist than have presently been confirmed.

Morrow's activities brought him into conflict with the law. He was brought before a court-martial in January 1919 charged with 'having in his possession without lawful authority, certain papers and writings, being copies of certain confidential documents belonging to government departments in order that he might publish their contents'. One might legitimately wonder if he had planned using them as inspiration for later cartoons or even postcards. In any case the authorities were sufficiently alarmed to commit the same Jack to Mountjoy Gaol.

John Killen's book included a Morrow card 'Catching Recruits', poking fun at army recruitment in Ireland. A further card entitled 'The Recruiting Sergeant' and signed 'Mac', dates from the pre-1910 era. Another, which seems to be from his hand, although unsigned, is entitled 'The Unemployed In Ireland' (**1.8**). It dates from 1906 and was also produced for the Dungannon Clubs. Known postcards of his from 1917 onwards include:

> 'Unconquerable' (**5. 9**)
> Britannia – 'Put these on like a good little boy and I'll promise you a nice
>   cake of land' (**3.14**)
> John Bull 'Here! Come on you, Get in.' (**TCD**)
> AOH/LOL 'Why can't you be a sensible man like ourselves?'
> 'On The Deck Of Patrick Lynch's Boat'
> 'In His Own Juice' (**TCD**)
> One Man's Land (**3.15**)
> Irish Ireland declines John Bull's invitation to the Irish Convention (**NLI**)

* Note: The (h) in modern typography represents a dot '·', e.g., ' ' placed over some Gaelic consonants.

Christine Spengler, 1945– : Spengler was probably the greatest twentieth century female war photographer and correspondent. She has worked for *Life*, *Paris Match*, *Newsweek*, *Time* and others. She was born in France although she grew up in Spain. Her work took her to many areas of conflict throughout the world, including Northern Ireland between 1970 and 1972. Although her photographs inevitably often featured soldiers, her work had a particular focus on the consequences of war on women and children. Sometimes the natural spirit and exuberance of children shone through the horror of conflict. In other cases the effects were much less positive. Her work often depicted the ordinary amongst the extraordinary. Two series of her photographs 'The Streets of Derry' and 'The Streets of Belfast' were produced as postcards. Her work is only featured fleetingly in this book (Conclusion **3**) as it was not predominantly political.

APPENDIX 2: PHOTOGRAPHERS

It would be readily accepted that photographers are of lesser importance than the artists who produced many of the postcards featured in this book. Some cards were the work of private individuals, since DIY postcard production was perfectly feasible from the early years of the twentieth century. Many however were the work of professional photographers, either working for their own businesses, for the press in a few cases, or for some of the large national companies. John Killen has already referred to Waltons and Boyds in Belfast. Some southern photographers should be added to the list.

Robert French, 1841–[?]: French was the leading photographer for about forty years up until 1914 for Lawrence's of Upper Sackville Street. They were probably the most important photographic studio in Ireland until the destruction of their business during the Easter Rising of 1916. French took many thousands of photographs for his employer. The vast majority of these were topographical.

However, a small number of pictures of evictions formed part of his vast portfolio. It was a very powerful and emotive issue, often highlighted by Irish nationalists. The Davitt Museum in County Mayo used two of his pictures of evictions in one of its promotional postcards featured in Chapter 9 of this book.

Brendan Keogh, 1887–[?]: He was principal photographer for Keogh Bros of Dorset Street and Stephens Green, a firm which remained in the business until 1958. His photographs include images and incidents of Home Rule rallies (e.g. no. **2.24**), of the 1916 Rising, and of elections in 1917, especially in Clare and Kilkenny. He also took photographs of Irish political personalities and incidents up until, and including the Irish Civil War. His work includes pictures of Fianna Éireann, De Valera, Michael Collins and Countess Markievicz. Much, although by no means all, of this was issued in postcard form. The National Library of Ireland has in its possession 232 glass negatives of his work.

W.D. Hogan: Hogan of Henry Street, Dublin, was a commercial and press photographer. He was active particularly in the period 1920 to 1935. Many of his pictures featured the Easter Rising and the Civil War. One of the larger groups of postcards was produced for Eason & Sons, and they showed much of the activity leading to the 1921 Truce and Treaty negotiations. Eason also published twelve of his photographs in a pamphlet entitled *Pictures of Dublin – After The Fighting June–July 1922*. He was also responsible for Civil War postcards featuring Limerick, which are now housed in the Limerick City Museum. No. **6.18** has been reproduced from that collection.

APPENDIX 3: VALUATION OF POSTCARDS

It is something of a truism to say that value is what a customer is prepared to pay. As with coins or china or almost any collectible, condition will be a major determinant of price. A card, which is dirty or badly creased, will have a much lower value than one in pristine condition. At the same time some allowance has to be made for age, and a little wear is acceptable. Where auctions are concerned, there will be very considerable price variations as much depends on who is present on the day.

There will always be a considerable margin between buying price and selling price. For the purposes of this piece, all prices quoted are replacement costs, which would equate also to insurance value. It should also be pointed out that there is generally little difference in value between mint or unposted and posted, or as some collectors would call them, 'postally used' cards, although the former are more likely to have been collected and cared for. Consequently, they will often be in better condition and therefore more expensive.

Modern cards, post 1969 are the cheapest available. Some commemorative issues, produced for museums are still available. For example, the picture of Thomas Russell can be purchased for under £1 from the Down County Museum in Downpatrick. Other commemorative issues, such as the republican and, to a lesser extent, loyalist cards of the 1970- and 1980s-era retail at between £2 and £10 for rarer examples. When we go into the market for works of the 'Golden Age', however, all these prices will seem ridiculously cheap.

The most numerous pre-1912 cards would appear to be those connected with the Belfast Strike of 1907. That is not so much that they are common, rather because a large range was produced. These cards average between about £35 to £40 each and are increasing in scarcity. Indeed, prices at about twice the level quoted are being asked by dealers in England.

Home Rule cards are fractionally cheaper than the normal strike cards. Good black and white cartoons are priced at around £25, while examples in colour fetch a small additional premium of around £5. Some rare photographic material could range a good deal higher in price. Recent trends show a widening gap between the relatively ordinary and scarcer examples, some of which now fetch three figure sums.

1916 Rising material is for the most part a little cheaper again. A largish range depicting leaders of varying importance would normally be priced in the £15 to £20 bracket. Again some rarer examples are a good deal more expensive. Some of the scenes of the damage in Dublin are fairly, though decreasingly common. They are still quite readily available for between £10 and £15. There is some rare material which could easily cost as much as £50.

Some of the First World War examples are comparable in price to the Home Rule stock, and would fall into the £15 to £20 price range. Two notable exceptions are the cards produced by the artist William Conor as fundraisers for the UVF Hospital in Belfast. They now fetch about double the price of others with a similar theme.

Anybody who can unearth any of the very early and rare Sinn Féin cards is most unlikely to accept less than £75 each. Other Sinn Féin, and similar issues, from the 1917–21 period are also quite expensive with at least £30 to £50 being charged for good examples. Irish Civil War material, which is pretty scarce, would fall within a similar price range, although this writer has witnessed a few extremely rare examples go at auction for three figure sums.

Political cards from the last three decades vary in price from about £3 to £10, but even these are becoming increasingly difficult to find. Probably the cheapest of these are reproductions of loyalist and republican murals at about £2 or even less, each. In recent years also, reproductions of some of the more popular loyalist and republican cards from the 'Golden Age' have been printed. For the most part, they are good quality copies, although in many cases their colours are richer than the original and the card itself is much lighter.

A dedicated deltiologist, to give a collector of postcards his/her correct title, will not be particularly interested in the modern facsimiles, but for someone seeking a cheaper entry to the hobby, they are a reasonable start. For somebody who sees these cards as interesting historical titbits, then the copies will be an affordable way of collecting. Like many of the other cards, prices of these have also risen and are still rising, but some examples are still available, costing between £1 and £2 each.

Postscript: For the last few years at least, the website www.vintagepostcards.com has had a very small selection of Sinn Féin, plus pro- and anti-Home Rule cards for sale at prices of between $150 and $250 each. Very few have sold! On the other hand some samples on eBay and in other auctions have far exceeded the average prices quoted here.

BIBLIOGRAPHY

The most important primary source material in this work is the postcards themselves. Most of the examples used are in private hands, but public collections have also been consulted and relevant samples have been reproduced. These include: the Linen Hall Library, Belfast, the Ulster Museum, the Samuels Collection in TCD, National Library of Ireland, Limerick City Museum and Valentine's Archive in St Andrews.

General Reference Works

Bennett, R., *The Black and Tans* (Four Square Books: London, 1961).

Connolly, S.J. (ed.), *The Oxford Companion To Irish History* (Oxford University Press: Oxford, 1998).

Dictionary of National Biography (D.N.B.), (Oxford University Press: Oxford, 1971).

Elliott, S. and Flackes, W.D., *Northern Ireland: A Political Directory* (Blackstaff Press: Belfast, 1999).

Hickey, D.J. and Doherty, J.E., *A Dictionary of Irish History Since 1800* (Gill & Macmillan: Dublin, 1980).

References for historical background and documentary extracts

Bamford F. and Bankes, V., *Vicious Circle* (Max Parrish: London, 1965).

Bardon, J., *Belfast: An Illustrated History* (Blackstaff Press: Belfast, 1983).

Bartlett, T., Dawson, K. and Keogh, D., *Rebellion: A Television History of 1798* (Gill & Macmillan: Dublin, 1998).

Buckland, P., *Irish Unionism 1885-1923: A Documentary History* (Stationery Office (for PRONI); Belfast, 1973).

Douglas, R., Harte, L. and O'Hara, J., *Drawing Conclusions: A Cartoon History of Anglo-Irish Relations 1798–1998* (Blackstaff Press: Belfast, 1998).

Downing, T. (ed.), *The Troubles: The background to the Question of Northern Ireland* (2nd edition) (Sphere: London 1982).

Dungan, M., *The Stealing of The Irish Crown Jewels: An Unsolved Crime* (Town House: Dublin, 2003).

Dutton, D., *'His Majesty's Loyal Opposition': The Unionist Party in Opposition 1905–1915* (Liverpool University Press: Liverpool, 1992).

Foy, M. and Barton B., *The Easter Rising* (Sutton Publishing Ltd: Stroud, 1999).

Gray, J., *City in Revolt: James Larkin and the Belfast Dockers Strike 1907* (Blackstaff Press: Belfast, 1985).

Jeffery, K., *Ireland and the Great War* (Cambridge University Press: Cambridge, 2000).

Lalor, B. (Gen. ed.), *The Encyclopaedia of Ireland* (Gill & Macmillan: Dublin, 2003).

Lee, J.J., *Ireland 1912–1985: Politics and Society* (Cambridge University Press: Cambridge, 1989).

Macardle, D., *The Irish Republic* (Irish Press: Dublin, 1951).

McBride, L.W. (ed.), *Images, Icons and the Irish Nationalist Imagination* (Four Courts Press: Dublin, 1999).

McCracken, D.P., *Forgotten Protest: Ireland and the Anglo-Boer War* (Ulster Historical Foundation, Belfast, 2003).

McKittrick, D., *et al*, *Lost Lives* (Mainstream Publishing: Edinburgh and London, 2004).

Novick, B., *Conceiving Revolution: Irish Nationalist Propaganda during the First World War* (Four Courts Press: Dublin, 2001).

O'Connor, N., *Cracking Crime: Jim Donovan – Forensic Detective* (O'Brien Press: Dublin, 2001).

O'Farrell, P., *Who's Who in The Irish War of Independence and Civil War, 1916–1923* (Lilliput Press: Dublin, 1997).

Rouse, S., *Into the Light: An Illustrated Guide to the Photographic Collections in the National Library of Ireland* (National Library of Ireland: Dublin, 1998).

Snoddy, T., *Dictionary of Irish Artists: Twentieth Century* (2nd edition) (Merlin Publishing: Dublin, 2002).

Spellissy, S., *The History of Limerick City* (Celtic Bookshop: Limerick, 1998).

Staunton, E., *The Nationalists of Northern Ireland, 1918–1973* (Columba Press: Dublin, 2001).

Stewart, A.T.Q., *The Summer Soldiers* (Blackstaff Press: Belfast, 1997).

Stewart, A.T.Q., *The Ulster Question* (Faber and Faber Ltd: London, 1967).

Stewart, A.T.Q., *Edward Carson* (Gill and Macmillan: Dublin, 1981).

On Postcards

Coysh, A.W., *The Dictionary of Picture Postcards in Britain, 1894–1939* (Antique Collectors' Club: Woodbridge, 1984).

Killen, J., *John Bull's Famous Circus: Ulster History through the Postcard 1905–1985* (O'Brien Press: Dublin, 1985).

Unpublished

O Conchubhair, P., 'Irish Political Cartoons', 1917, Morrow, National Library of Ireland, Ir 94108 M18.

Contemporary newspapers and journals
Belfast Newsletter (An Ulster unionist viewpoint)
Irish News (A nationalist viewpoint)
Irish Times (A government/unionist viewpoint)
The Republic (Dungannon Clubs/Republican viewpoint)

Catalogue
Picture Postcard Values 2012 (some limited information on pricing of Irish
    political cards.)

Articles
Brady, T.J., 'Postcards and History' in *History Today* (Dec. 1969).
Ryan, P.J., 'The Fourth Siege of Limerick: Civil War 1922' in *The Old Limerick
    Journal*, No. 38 (Winter 2002).
Skehan, J., 'Who Stole the Crown Jewels?' in *Ireland of the Welcomes* (Mar.–Apr.
    1976).

The internet was consulted fleetingly in researching Valentine's cards, but the only
information of any substance used was on the YCVI, Margaretta D'Arcy and the
Chernobyl Children's Project.

The website bureauofmilitaryhistory.ie was also consulted briefly.

INDEX

Aberdeen, Lord, Lord Lieutenant, 9
Act of Union, 52, 79, 149, 150
Adair, Sir William, 109
Aer Lingus, 128
Albert Clock, 36, 38
Anti-Partition League, 128
Antrim and 1798, 147, 148
Antrim, Earl of, 141
Ancient Order of Hibernians, 37
Apprentice Boys (of Derry), 112, 141
Ardnacrusha, 129, 130
Arden, John, 135
Army Powers Act 1922, 126
Ashe, Thomas, 72, 73, 74, 77, 82, 83, 97
Ashbourne (Co. Meath), 72, 73
Askew, Norman, British Nuclear Fuels, 138
Asquith Sir H., MP., 22, 78, 80, 161
Auxiliaries, 91, 95, 99
Aud, The, 62

Bagally, Captain, 97
Baird (publisher), 148, 156
Ballynahinch, Co. Down, 148, 149
Balmoral Showgrounds, 28
Bamforth & Co. (publisher), 53, 131
Bangor, 31
Barrett, Constable, 16
Barrett, Richard, 126
Béal na mBláth, 106
Belfast Agreement, 135
Belfast City Hall, 35
Belfast Protestant Association, 18
Belfast Newsletter, 5, 3, 15, 16
Belfast Strike (1907), 13–18, 179
Belfast Telegraph, 111, 175
Belgium, 85
Benburb, Battle of, 3
Birrell, Augustine, 93
Black and Tans, 91, 95–7
Black Cross (Anarchist), 128
Blackpool, 131
Blair, Tony, 138
Blaris, 147
Bloody Sunday 1920, 97
Bloody Sunday 1972, 113, 115, 163, and
    Initiative and Justice Campaign, 164

Boer War, 2,3
Bonar, Law A., MP., 160
Boyne, Battle of the, 140, 142, 143
Buncrana, 131
Bradford, Rev. Robert, M.P., 120,121
Brewster, Gordon (artist), 78–80, 85, 86, 90,
    93, 102, 162, 174
Britannia, 11, 58, 59
Brugha, Cathal, 94, 104, 105
Bruton, John, 135
Buckingham Palace Conference, 49
Burke, Edmund, 144–6
Byrne, Bobby, 94, 95, 97

Cambrai, Battle of, 57
Carbery, Eithne, 148
Carey, J.W. (artist), 148
Carrickfergus, Co. Antrim, 36, 142
Carron, Owen, M.P., 164
Carson, Sir Edward, 23, 25, 28, 34, 40,
    49–52, 76, 108
Caryll, 3rd Viscount Maryborough, 143
Casement, Sir Roger, 62
Casey, Bishop, 137
Castlereagh, Lord (Robert Stewart), 140,
    148–50
Catholic Association, 151, 152
Catholic Emancipation, 151, 152
Celbridge, Co. Kildare, 4
Charles (HRH Prince of Wales) and Diana
    (Princess of Wales), 116, 138
Chernobyl (Childrens Project), 137, 183
Churchill, Winston, M.P., 29
Clancy, G., 98, 99
Clare, Co. East, 81, 82
Clemenceau, G., 7, 60
Clarke, Thomas, 1, 71
Clontarf rally, 152
Colbert, Cornelius (Con), 71, 72
Collins, Michael, 92, 102, 106, 178
Communist Party of Ireland, 104
Conor, William (artist), 54, 55, 180
Confederation of Kilkenny, 3
Congo, 139
Connaught Rangers, 54
Connolly, James, 62, 68, 69, 140, 154, 155

Conor, William (artist), 54, 55, 180
Coogan, Tim Pat, 99
Cork, 97, 98
Corry, Sam, 111
Cosgrave, William, 82
Countercards of Pontefract (publisher), 135
Corunna, Battle of, 19
Craig, Sir James, 109, 127
Craig, William, M.P., 121
Crawford, Frederick, 30
Cromwell, Oliver, 3
Cúchulainn, 169, 170, 173
Cumann na mBan, 75
Cumann na nGaedheal, 2, 151, 166
Curragh Mutiny, 29, 30
Currans (publisher), 63
Curran, Sarah, 151

Dáil, 91–4, 135, 155
Daily Chronicle, 16
Daily Express, 82, 175
Daily Mail, 55, 157
Daily Sketch, 63, 69, 82
Daily Telegraph, 96
D'Arcy, Margaretta, 134–5, 183
Davis, Thomas, 79
Davitt, Michael, 153
Derry (Londonderry) Seige, 8, 16, 36, 121,
    123, 141, 144
De Valera, 60, 77, 82, 101, 102, 125, 129,
    139, 178
Devine, Michael, 118
Devlin, Joe, M.P., 18, 19, 36, 86, 109, 110
Devoy, John, 1
Dillon, John, 36, 79, 81, 86
Donaghadee, Co. Down, 31
Donegall Place, 35, 36
Donegore Hill, 147
DORA (Defence Of The Realm Act), 56–8,
    73, 86, 162
Douglas, James, xi
Down County and 1798, 148, 149
Downpatrick Gaol, 150
Doyle, John, 99
Drogheda, Siege of, 3
Drumcree, 170
Dublin Castle, 7, 63, 68, 77, 79
Dublin Fusiliers, 54
Dublin Metropolitan Police, 3

Dublin Transvaal Committee, 2
Dungannon Clubs, 2, 4, 5, 7, 10–13, 148, 176
Dunne, Reginald, 126, 127

Eason (publisher), 12, 101, 105, 178
Edward VIII, 8, 10
Éire, 60
Electricity Supply Act, 1927, 129, 130
Emmett, Robert, 150, 151
ESB, 129
Eucharistic Congress, 1932, 131, 132,

Fenians, 1
Fianna Éireann, 75, 155, 178
Fianna Fáil, 151
First World War, 13, 34, 49–61, 69, 113,
    147, 162, 166, 175, 176, 180
Fitzgerald, Lord Edward, 146
Fitzgerald, Garrett, 133, 134
Fitzharris, James, aka 'Skin the Goat', 36
Fitzpatrick, Thomas, aka 'Spot', 174
Four Courts, 102, 103, 133
Fox, Charles James, 145
Frederick, Duke of Schomberg, 142
Freeman's Journal, The, 7
French, Robert (photographer), 178
French, Sir John, 57
Friers, Rowel (artist), 111–12, 175
Frongoch, 70

GAA, 14
Gaelic League, 4
Gallaher's (tobacco factory), 10
Gallaher, Thomas, 14
Gallipoli, 50
George III, 144
George IV, 8
George V, 2, 8, 107
George (Prince of Denmark), 143
Germany, 49
Gladstone, William, 5, 154
Glasgow, 92, 96
Gow, Andrew Carrick (artist), 143
Government of Ireland Act 1920, 108
Gough, Sir Hubert, 29, 30
Green Cross, 163
Griffith, Arthur, 2, 12, 60, 82, 86, 88, 89

Haddington Road, Dublin, 64
Haicéad Padraigín, 3
Hammam Hotel, 104
Hastings, Warren (Gov. Gen. of India), 145
Haughey, Charles, 133, 134
Hely's (publisher), 63, 69, 156, 157
Hogan, W.D., (photographer), 92, 105, 178
Home Rule Bills, 1, 18, 21, 22–48, 49, 59,
    61, 157, 159, 166, 167, 176, 178, 179,
    167, 168

Ingram, John Kells, 148
Inghinidhe na hÉireann, 2
INLA, 118
Inner Temple, 144
Inniskillings, 54
Irish Christian Brothers, 6
Irish Citizen Army, 62, 75, 155
Irish Civil War, 103, 107, 178, 180
Irish Convention 1917–18, 87, 161
Irish Council Bill, 7
Irish Free State, 91, 125
Irish Guards, 54
Irish Independent, 175
Irish National Aid, 162
Irish National Congress, 135
Irish News, 110, 130
Irish Parliamentry Party, 7, 12, 22, 78, 85, 87,
    161, 162, 165, 166
IRA, 91, 99, 101, 114, 118, 135
Irish Times, 10, 16, 130
Irish Volunteers, 26, 27, 51, 75, 77, 91
Irish War News, 68, 130
Irish Weekly Independent, 174
Irish Women's Franchise League, 47
Irish Women's Suffrage Federation, 47
Irish Worker, The, 78, 175
Irregulars, 92, 103, 105

James II, 123, 140, 143, 144

Kaiser, The, 51
Kavanagh, Art (artist), 95
Kavanagh, Ernest, 175
Kent (Ceannt), Edmund, 71
Keogh, Brendan, 178
Kilkenny Co. & City, 82

Kilmainham, 72, 74
Kilmorna, 9
Kingstown (Dún Laoghaire), 64
Kinsale, 143

Land Act (Gladstone's 1881), 154
Land Act (Wyndham), 5, 6
Land League, 140, 153
Larkin, James, 13, 17, 18
Larne gun-running, 22, 31, 108, 109
Lawrences, 47, 178
Leader, The, 2
League of Nations, 139
Lebanon, 139
Lennon, Maggie, 17
Lewis Gaol, 82
Liberty League, 89
Limerick 'Soviet', 94, 95
Lincoln Gaol, 94
Listowel, Co. Kerry, 9
Liverpool, 13
Lloyd George, David, 56, 92, 93, 101, 108
London Opinion, 175
Longford Co., 81, 82
Long Kesh aka The Maze, 117
Louis XVI, 145
Louth, Co., 16
Loyal National Appeal Association, 152
Lowe, General, 70
LPOW (Loyalist Prisoners of War), 170
Lynch, Liam, 92

MacCready, Gen. GOC, 101, 108
Mac Curtain, Tomás, 96
Mac Neill, Eoin, 62
MacSwiney, Terence, 96, 97
Manchester Martyrs, 131
Mansion House, 93, 100, 101
Markievicz, Countess (Constance
    Gore-Booth), 155, 178
Maxwell, Gen., 74, 75
McBride, Maud Gonne, 12, 36
McBride, Major John, 36
McCracken, Henry Joy, 147
McDonagh, Thomas, 71
McGill, Donald (artist), 45, 46, 175–6
McGuinness, Joseph, 82
McKelvey, Joseph, 126

McMullan, Charles, 17, 19
Meagher, Thomas Francis, 152
Mellows, Liam, 126
Military Service Bill, 77
Milner, Lord, 30
Mitchel, John, 79
Molly Maguires, 37
Monks, George, 176
Mountjoy Prison, 83, 97, 177
Mount St Bridge, Dublin, 64
Moore, Sir John, 19, 20
Moran, Denis, 2
Morrow, Jack, 59, 60, 176
Munro, Henry, 148
Munster Republic, 92, 105
Munster Rifles, 54
Murray, Noel and Marie, 128, 129

Napoleon, 19, 150
Nation, The, 148, 174
National Council, 82, 89
Nelson's Pillar, 111, 112
New Ireland, 107, 177
Nicaragua, 137
North, Lord, 145
Nugent, Major-General, 147, 149

O'Callaghan, Michael, 98
Ó Cearnaigh, Peadar, 57
O'Connell, Daniel, 46, 79, 140, 151, 152
O'Connor, Rory, 126
O'Donovan Rossa, Jeremiah, 1, 82
O'Dwyer, Bishop of Limerick, 7, 74, 87, 161
O'Flanagan, Fr Michael, 89
Oglaigh na hÉireann, 75
O'Hanrahans, 174
O'Higgins, Kevin, 125, 126
O'Kelly, Sean T., 60
O Leary. John, 1
O'Mahony, Pierce Gun, 8, 9
O'Neill, Henry (of Shanes Castle), 144
O'Neill, Lady aka Lady Molyneux, 143
O'Neill, Sir Neil, 144
O Neill, Owen Roe, 3
O Rahilly, The, 2
O'Shea, Kitty, 8, 18, 175
O'Sullivan, Joseph, 126, 127
Our Boys, 176

Palestine, 50
Parnell, Charles Stuart, 2, 8, 18, 153, 174
Partridge, Bernard, 84
Pearse, Patrick, 63, 68, 70, 154, 169, 170
Peel, Sir Robert, 152
Pitt, William, 145
Plunkett, Joseph, 60, 81
Plunkett, Count, 60, 61, 81, 89, 90
Portmagee, 133
Powell Press, 63, 71, 74, 99
Public Safety Acts (1923, 1924, 1926), 126
Punch, 47, 84, 93, 174

Quiz, 174

Raemaekers, Louis (cartoonist), 54
Randalstown, Co. Antrim, 147
Reagan, President Ronald, 135–7
Redmond, John, 6, 7, 22, 33, 34, 36–8, 41, 46,
    49–53, 56, 76, 78–81, 86, 87, 161, 175
Redmond, Willie, 82
Redshanks, 141
Representation of the People Act 1918, 79
Republic, The, 1, 6, 10, 11, 173
Reynolds, Garda Michael, 128
RIC, 13–15, 91, 95, 105, 106, 160
Roche, Adi, 137
Royal Irish Regiment, 2
Rinuccini, Cardinal, 3
Robinson & Cleavers, 36
Rockingham, Lord (Charles Watson-
    Wentworth), 144, 145
Roscommon, Co., 6
Rotary (publisher), 23, 63, 69
Royal Hibernian Academy, 174
RUC, 109, 119
Russell, Thomas, 150, 151, 179

Sackville St (O'Connell St), 69, 92, 103, 104
Salisbury, Lord, 160
San Salvador, 137
Sands, Bobby, 116, 117, 163
Sartre, Jean Paul, 128
Schomberg, Duke of, see Frederick, Duke of
    Schomberg
Second World War, 107, 110, 130
Sellafield, 137

Sheares, John & Henry, 146–7
Sheehy-Skeffington, Hannah, 47
Sherwood Foresters, 64
Singleton, Major, 55
Sinn Féin, 4, 5, 12, 49, 56, 58, 60, 61, 73,
    75–91, 93, 97, 102, 109, 127, 155, 161,
    164, 166, 174, 180
Sloan, Thomas, 18–21
Solemn League and Covenant, 22, 77
Soloheadbeg, Co.Tipperary, 91
Spencer, Earl, 26, 27, 160
Spender, Wilfrid Lt-Col., 108, 109
Spengler, Christine, 169, 177
St Michans, 146, 147
Sunday Business Post, 119
Sunday Independent, 134, 174
Swift, Dean, 11
Swinburne, A.C., 32
Syndicalism, 34

Thatcher, Margaret (Maggie), 116, 136
Times, The, 55
Tipperary, Co., 91
Toby, 111
Townsend, T.H., 93
Trinity College Dublin, 69, 70, 144
Tyrconnell, Earl of (Richard Talbot), 141, 144

UDA, 7
Ulster Clubs, 7
Ulster Custom, 9
Ulster Division, 3
Ulster Unionist Council, 6
Ulster Unionists, 6, 7, 22, 30, 62, 77, 89,
    159, 166
Ulster Rifles, 54
United Irish League, 2, 6
United Irishmen, 146
United National Societies Committee, 2

United Nations, 139
USC 'Specials', 107, 120
UVF, 22, 26, 51, 108, 160

Valentia Island, 132
Valentine's (publisher), 43, 63, 69, 156, 181,
    183
Vanguard, 121
Versailles, 3
Vicars, Sir Arthur, 8, 9
Vienna Congress (1815), 150
Viviani, M., 87
Volunteers (1780), 51,52

Walsh, J.J., 174
Wandsworth Prison, 126,
Wellington, Duke of (Arthur Wellesley), 152
Wendover, 144
West Belfast Constituency, 109
Westminster Parliament, 12, 21, 39, 42, 52,
    86, 91, 92, 95
Wexford, Siege of, 3
Whelan, Thomas, 97, 98
William III, Prince of Orange, 141–143
William IV, 8
Wilson, President Woodrow, 60
Wilson, Sir Henry, 126
Wolfe, Rev. Charles, 20
Wolfe Tone, Theobald, 79
Workers Republic, The, 104
Wyndham Land Act, see Land Act
    (Wyndham)

YCVI, 27–9, 183
Young Ireland, 79, 80
Young Irelanders, 148, 153
Ypres 70